Contents

BLACKENED CHICKEN 8

SPICY THAI BASIL CHICKEN (PAD KRAPOW GAI) 8

ONE PAN ORECCHIETTE PASTA 9

AVOCADO SALSA AND SARDINE FRENCHY 10

CALIFORNIA BOUNTY BEEF AND VEGETABLE NOODLES 11

BUCATINI ALL'AMATRICIANA 11

EASY AND SPICY THAI BASIL CHICKEN WITH EGG 12

MISO-GLAZED BLACK COD 13

MUSHROOM SPINACH OMELET 14

CRAB-STUFFED LOBSTER TAIL 14

BROWN RICE BREAKFAST PORRIDGE 15

BAKED SALMON 16

CREAMY CAJUN CHICKEN PASTA 16

CAJUN CHICKEN PASTA 17

DELICIOUS BLACK BEAN BURRITOS 18

CHICKEN PARMIGIANA 19

FILET MIGNON WITH RICH BALSAMIC GLAZE 19

SAVORY GARLIC MARINATED STEAKS 20

STUFFED PEPPERS MY WAY 21

CHICKEN MARSALA 22

OVEN BBQ CHICKEN DRUMSTICKS 23

MAMA'S BEST BROILED TOMATO SANDWICH 23

PEANUT NOODLES 24

GRILLED FISH STEAKS 25

ASPARAGUS AND MOZZARELLA STUFFED CHICKEN BREASTS 25

CHICKEN SCARPARIELLO 26

QUICK GNOCCHI 27

BAKED SPLIT CHICKEN BREAST 27

GRILLED ROCK LOBSTER TAILS 28

EASY MARINATED PORK TENDERLOIN 28

PORK TENDERLOIN DIABLO 29

BROILED SCALLOPS 30

GRILLED PORK LOIN CHOPS 30

BROCCOLI AND CHICKEN STIR-FRY 31

CHICKEN AND MUSHROOMS 32

MARINATED RANCH BROILED CHICKEN 33

BROILED LOBSTER TAILS 33

LEMON ROSEMARY SALMON 34

PARMESAN SAGE PORK CHOPS 34

BACON MUSHROOM CHICKEN 35

EMERGENCY CHICKEN 36

FISH IN FOIL 36

CHICKEN WITH LEMON-CAPER SAUCE 37

ACAPULCO CHICKEN 38

HONEY GRILLED SHRIMP 39

SPAGHETTI AGLIO E OLIO 39

SALMON WITH TOMATOES 40

PEANUT BUTTER AND BANANA FRENCH TOAST 41

POTATO SKILLET 41

PARMESAN-CRUSTED PORK CHOPS 42

CHICKEN, ASPARAGUS, AND MUSHROOM SKILLET 43

GNOCCHI WITH SAGE-BUTTER SAUCE 43

BLUE CHEESE, BACON AND CHIVE STUFFED PORK CHOPS 44

SIMPLE LEMON HERB CHICKEN 45

DOMINICAN STYLE OATMEAL 45

FAVORITE BARBECUE CHICKEN 46

PORK FRIED RICE 47

CHICKEN BREASTS WITH CHIPOTLE GREEN ONION GRAVY 47

SIMPLE STROMBOLI 48

SALMON 49

TOMATO BASIL SALMON 50

SAUSAGE-STUFFED EGGPLANT 50

SPOILED BABY BACK RIBS 51

FIRE ROASTED TOMATO AND FETA PASTA WITH SHRIMP 52

MEN LOVE THIS STEAK 52

FETA AND BACON STUFFED CHICKEN WITH ONION MASHED POTATOES 53

ONION PAN-FRIED PORK CHOPS 54

CREAMY CHEESY SCRAMBLED EGGS WITH BASIL 55

PAN SEARED RED SNAPPER 55

SLOW COOKER SPICY CHICKEN 56

EASY YET ROMANTIC FILET MIGNON 57

VERACRUZ-STYLE RED SNAPPER 57

MAPLE CAJUN MAHI MAHI 58

SPAGHETTI ALLA CARBONARA 59

EGGPLANT SANDWICHES 59

BAKED FALAFEL 60

MUSTARD CRUSTED TILAPIA 61

GARLIC CHICKEN FRIED BROWN RICE 61

LUCKY'S QUICKIE CHICKIE 62

GORGONZOLA STUFFED CHICKEN BREASTS WRAPPED IN BACON 63

DRUNKEN MUSSELS 64

QUICK LEMON DIJON CHICKEN 64

SEXY SHRIMP SCAMPI 65

PAN SEARED LEMON TILAPIA WITH PARMESAN PASTA 65

CRAB LEGS WITH GARLIC BUTTER SAUCE 66

CORIANDER AND CUMIN RUBBED PORK CHOPS 67

PIZZA CHICKEN 67

CHANA MASALA (SAVORY INDIAN CHICK PEAS) 68

SPICY SALMON WITH CARAMELIZED ONIONS 69

A PAD THAI WORTH MAKING 70

JALAPENO POPPER GRILLED CHEESE SANDWICH 71

POTATO CAKE 72

STUFFED EGGPLANT WITH SHRIMP AND BASIL 72

CHICKEN SCALLOPINI 73

DELICIOUS GRILLED HAMBURGERS 74

COLA ONION PORK CHOPS 74

ALTERNATIVE BAKED SALMON 75

VEGETARIAN BIBIMBAP 76

PHYLLO-WRAPPED HALIBUT FILLETS WITH LEMON SCALLION SAUCE 76

GRILLED MONGOLIAN PORK CHOPS 77

FETA AND SUN-DRIED TOMATO STUFFED CHICKEN 78

LOBSTER TAILS STEAMED IN BEER 79

BAKED TOFU 80

LONDON BROIL 80

HONEY SOY TILAPIA 81

ACCIDENTAL FISH 82

STIR-FRY PORK WITH GINGER 82

ORANGE, HONEY AND SOY CHICKEN 83

CHICKEN MASSAMAN CURRY 84

LEMON GARLIC CHICKEN 84

STIR-FRY PORK WITH GINGER 85

LIME-MARINATED MAHI MAHI 86

SAUTEED SCALLOPS 86

WILD RICE AND ASPARAGUS CHICKEN BREASTS 87

SLOPPY JOE SANDWICHES 87

PAN-POACHED ALASKAN SALMON PICCATA 88

TENDER TOMATO CHICKEN BREASTS 89

FRENCH EGG AND BACON SANDWICH 90

STIR-FRY CHICKEN AND VEGETABLES 90

LOW CARB PANCAKE CREPES 91

BROWN SUGAR HAM STEAK 92

SPICY GRILLED CHEESE SANDWICH 92

ONE-DISH ROCKFISH 93

QUICK EGGPLANT PARMESAN 93

RILLED SALMON WITH BACON AND CORN RELISH 94

TROUT AMANDINE 95

MINUTE STEAKS WITH BARBEQUE BUTTER SAUCE 96

KETO CHICKEN PARMESAN 96

SEAFOOD SANDWICH 97

LEMON GARLIC SALMON 98

GREEK COUSCOUS 99

SASSY STEAK MARINADE AND SAUCE 99

CHINESE SPARERIBS 100

MEDITERRANEAN TILAPIA 101

SALMON IN PARCHMENT 102

PASTA MELANZANA 102

HOW TO COOK TROUT... 103

BLUEBERRY LEMON BREAKFAST QUINOA 104

MALAYSIAN MANGO CHICKEN CURRY... 104

SOUTHERN FRIED CATFISH.. 105

JOEL'S JERK CHICKEN PINEAPPLE PASTA 106

ASHLEY'S CHICKEN KATSU WITH TONKATSU SAUCE 107

BBQ TUNA FRITTERS 108

JUICY BUTT STEAKS 108

STICKY GARLIC PORK CHOPS 109

BLACK BEAN BREAKFAST BOWL 110

SALSA BISCUIT CHICKEN 110

PROSCIUTTO-WRAPPED CHERRY-STUFFED CHICKEN BREASTS 111

ALOHA CHICKEN BURGERS 112

DAN'S FAVORITE CHICKEN SANDWICH.. 113

ROASTED VEGGIE PASTA 114

EASY SPICY MEXICAN-AMERICAN CHICKEN 115

VERMICELLI NOODLE BOWL... 115

ASIAN CARRYOUT NOODLES 116

ROASTED TURKEY LEGS 117

BROWN RICE BREAKFAST PORRIDGE 118

SAVANNAH'S BEST MARINATED PORTOBELLO MUSHROOMS 118

SALMON MANGO BANGO.. 119

FRUITY GRILLED PORK TENDERLOIN... 119

NEW ORLEANS BARBEQUED SHRIMP 120

E-Z MARINATED SWORDFISH 121

MOZZARELLA MUSHROOM CHICKEN... 121

HAM AND CHICKEN CASSEROLE.. 122

VEAL CHOP WITH PORTABELLO MUSHROOMS.. 123

ZUCCHINI E POMODORI GRATINATI (ZUCCHINI AND TOMATO GRATIN) 123

GRILLED SALMON STEAKS WITH SAVORY BLUEBERRY SAUCE........................... 124

SEA BASS A LA MICHELE.. 125

RISOTTO WITH CHICKEN AND ASPARAGUS.. 126

TERIYAKI RIB EYE STEAKS.. 127

STUFFED PORK CHOPS WITH GORGONZOLA AND APPLE 127

BEEF AND MUSHROOM STUFFED PEPPERS 128

CREAMY COTTAGE CHEESE SCRAMBLED EGGS 129

BAKED SHELLS IN SAUCE 130

BLACKENED CHICKEN

Servings: 2 | Prep: 10m | Cooks: 10m | Total: 20m

NUTRITION FACTS

Calories: 135.1 | Carbohydrates: 0.9g | Protein: 24.7g | Cholesterol: 67.2mg | Sodium: 204.7mg

INGREDIENTS

- 1/2 teaspoon paprika
- 1/8 teaspoon salt
- 1/4 teaspoon cayenne pepper
- 1/4 teaspoon ground cumin
- 1/4 teaspoon dried thyme
- 1/8 teaspoon ground white pepper
- 1/8 teaspoon onion powder
- 2 skinless, boneless chicken breast halves

DIRECTIONS

1. Preheat oven to 350 degrees F (175 degrees C). Lightly grease a baking sheet. Heat a cast iron skillet over high heat for 5 minutes until it is smoking hot.
2. Mix together the paprika, salt, cayenne, cumin, thyme, white pepper, and onion powder. Oil the chicken breasts with cooking spray on both sides, then coat the chicken breasts evenly with the spice mixture.
3. Place the chicken in the hot pan, and cook for 1 minute. Turn, and cook 1 minute on other side. Place the breasts on the prepared baking sheet.
4. Bake in the preheated oven until no longer pink in the center and the juices run clear, about 5 minutes.

SPICY THAI BASIL CHICKEN (PAD KRAPOW GAI)

Servings: 2 | Prep: 15m | Cooks: 10m | Total: 25m

NUTRITION FACTS

Calories: 715 | Carbohydrates: 58.6g | Protein: 49.8g | Cholesterol: 155.9mg | Sodium: 1181.9mg

INGREDIENTS

- 1/3 cup chicken broth
- 1 tablespoon oyster sauce
- 1 pound skinless, boneless chicken thighs, coarsely chopped
- 1/4 cup sliced shallots

- 1 tablespoon soy sauce, or as needed
- 2 teaspoons fish sauce
- 1 teaspoon white sugar
- 1 teaspoon brown sugar
- 2 tablespoons vegetable oil
- 4 cloves garlic, minced
- 2 tablespoons minced Thai chilies, Serrano, or other hot pepper
- 1 cup very thinly sliced fresh basil leaves
- 2 cups hot cooked rice

DIRECTIONS

1. Whisk chicken broth, oyster sauce, soy sauce, fish sauce, white sugar, and brown sugar together in a bowl until well blended.
2. Heat large skillet over high heat. Drizzle in oil. Add chicken and stir fry until it loses its raw color, 2 to 3 minutes. Stir in shallots, garlic, and sliced chilies. Continue cooking on high heat until some of the juices start to caramelize in the bottom of the pan, about 2 or 3 more minutes. Add about a tablespoon of the sauce mixture to the skillet; cook and stir until sauce begins to caramelize, about 1 minute.
3. Pour in the rest of the sauce. Cook and stir until sauce has deglazed the bottom of the pan. Continue to cook until sauce glazes onto the meat, 1 or 2 more minutes. Remove from heat.
4. Stir in basil. Cook and stir until basil is wilted, about 20 seconds. Serve with rice.

ONE PAN ORECCHIETTE PASTA

Servings: 2 | Prep: 15m | Cooks: 25m | Total: 40m

NUTRITION FACTS

Calories: 662 | Carbohydrates: 46.2g | Fat: 39.1g | Protein: 31.2g | Cholesterol: 60mg | Sodium: 1360mg

INGREDIENTS

- 2 tablespoons olive oil
- 1/2 onion, diced
- salt to taste
- 8 ounces spicy Italian sausages, casings removed
- 3 1/2 cups low-sodium chicken broth, divided, or as needed
- 1 1/4 cups orecchiette pasta, or more to taste
- 1/2 cup roughly chopped arugula, or to taste
- 1/4 cup finely grated Parmigiano-Reggiano cheese, or to taste

DIRECTIONS

1. Heat olive oil in a large, deep skillet over medium heat. Cook and stir onion with a pinch of salt in hot oil until onion is soft and golden, 5 to 7 minutes. Stir sausage into onions; cook and stir until sausage is broken up and browned, 5 to 7 minutes.
2. Pour 1 1/2 cups chicken broth into sausage mixture and bring to a boil while scraping the browned bits of food off of the bottom of the pan with a wooden spoon. Add orecchiette pasta; cook and stir pasta in hot broth, adding remaining broth when liquid is absorbed, until pasta is cooked through and most of the broth is absorbed, about 15 minutes.
3. Stir arugula into pasta-sausage mixture until arugula wilts. Ladle pasta into bowls and dust with Parmigiano-Reggiano cheese.

AVOCADO SALSA AND SARDINE FRENCHY
Servings: 4 | Prep: 15m | Cooks: 10m | Total: 25m

NUTRITION FACTS

Calories: 274.5 | Carbohydrates: 26g | Protein: 12.9g | Cholesterol: 25.4mg | Sodium: 923.9mg

INGREDIENTS

- 1 avocado, mashed
- 2 romaine lettuce leaves, chopped
- 1/4 green bell pepper, finely chopped
- 1 teaspoon lemon juice
- 4 slices French bread
- 2 teaspoons extra-virgin olive oil
- 1 (4.375 ounce) can canned sardines in water, drained
- 1 (14.5 ounce) can diced tomatoes with basil, garlic, and oregano - drained

DIRECTIONS

1. Preheat oven to 350 degrees F (175 degrees C).
2. Combine avocado, chopped lettuce, chopped green pepper, and lemon juice in a small bowl.
3. Brush extra-virgin olive oil on bread slices and toast in the preheated oven until browned, about 5 minutes on each side.
4. Remove bread slices from oven. Spread with avocado mixture; top with sardines and canned tomatoes.

CALIFORNIA BOUNTY BEEF AND VEGETABLE NOODLES

Servings: 2 | Prep: 30m | Cooks: 16m | Total: 51m | Additional: 5m

NUTRITION FACTS

Calories: 588.8 | Carbohydrates: 15.3g | Protein: 23.8g | Cholesterol: 85.6mg | Sodium: 877mg

INGREDIENTS

- 1/2 pound beef sirloin steak
- 1/2 teaspoon garlic salt
- 1/2 teaspoon freshly ground black pepper
- 3 tablespoons olive oil, divided
- 2 eaches Mexican squash
- 1/3 large carrot
- 2 radishes
- 1/2 avocado, diced
- 1/2 cup grape tomatoes, halved
- ¼ cup chopped cilantro
- 1/2 cup sour cream
- 1 tablespoon sriracha sauce

DIRECTIONS

1. Season steak with garlic salt and black pepper.
2. Heat 1 tablespoon olive oil in a large skillet over medium-high heat. Add steak; cook until browned, 4 to 5 minutes per side. Transfer steak to a cutting board and let rest, about 5 minutes. Slice into thin strips.
3. Cut Mexican squash, carrot, and radishes into noodles using a spiralizer.
4. Heat remaining 2 tablespoons oil in the skillet over medium heat. Add carrot noodles; cook and stir until lightly browned, about 3 minutes. Add squash noodles; cook, stirring constantly, until tender, about 5 minutes.
5. Divide carrot and squash noodle mixture between 2 serving plates. Top with sliced steak. Garnish with radish noodles, avocado, grape tomatoes, and cilantro.
6. Whisk sour cream and sriracha sauce together in a small bowl. Drizzle over serving plates.

BUCATINI ALL'AMATRICIANA

Servings: 2 | Prep: 10m | Cooks: 29m | Total: 39m

NUTRITION FACTS

Calories: 633.9 | Carbohydrates: 60.1g | Protein: 17.3g | Cholesterol: 21.9mg | Sodium: 478.1mg

INGREDIENTS

- 5 ounces bucatini pasta
- 1/4 cup extra-virgin olive oil
- 3 eaches crushed garlic cloves
- 1 1/2 ounces guanciale (cured pork cheek), sliced
- 1/4 cup sliced red onion
- 1 pinch red pepper flakes
- 1/2 (8 ounce) can crushed San Marzano tomatoes
- 1 pinch salt and ground black pepper to taste
- 1 ounce freshly grated Pecorino Romano cheese

DIRECTIONS

1. Fill a large pot with lightly salted water and bring to a rolling boil. Stir in bucatini and return to a boil. Cook, uncovered, stirring occasionally, until bucatini is tender, about 11 minutes. Drain.
2. Heat oil in a large skillet over medium-high heat. Add garlic cloves; cook until golden brown, about 1 minute. Remove with a slotted spoon and discard. Add guanciale; cook and stir until crisp and golden, about 4 minutes. Add onion and red pepper flakes; cook and stir until onion is translucent, about 3 minutes. Stir in tomatoes, salt, and black pepper. Simmer tomato sauce until flavors combine, about 10 minutes.
3. Stir bucatini and Pecorino Romano cheese into tomato sauce and toss until evenly coated.

EASY AND SPICY THAI BASIL CHICKEN WITH EGG

Servings: 2 | Prep: 10m | Cooks: 15m | Total: 25m

NUTRITION FACTS

Calories: 312.1 | Carbohydrates: 38.6g | Protein: 22.6g | Cholesterol: 218.3mg | Sodium: 1113.1mg

INGREDIENTS

- 1 serving cooking spray
- 2 eggs
- 1 1/2 cups cooked white rice
- 2 eaches Thai chile peppers, or more to taste
- 2 cloves garlic, peeled, or more to taste
- 1 chicken breast half, cut into bite-size pieces
- 2 tablespoons soy sauce
- 2 tablespoons oyster sauce
- 1 teaspoon white sugar
- 14 leaves Thai basil

DIRECTIONS

1. Coat a skillet with cooking spray and place over medium heat; cook and stir eggs until scrambled and set, about 5 minutes. Divide rice between 2 bowls and add eggs to rice.
2. Grind Thai chile peppers and garlic together with a mortar and pestle or in a food processor.
3. Coat skillet with cooking spray and heat over medium-high heat; cook and stir pepper-garlic mixture until fragrant and garlic is golden brown, about 1 minute. Add chicken; cook and stir until chicken is about halfway-cooked, about 3 minutes.
4. Mix soy sauce, oyster sauce, and sugar into chicken; cook and stir until chicken is no longer pink in the center, about 3 minutes more. Add basil and stir for 10 seconds. Remove skillet from heat and continue stirring mixture until basil is wilted; spoon over rice and egg.

MISO-GLAZED BLACK COD

Servings: 2 | Prep: 10m | Cooks: 15m | Total: 40m | Additional: 15m

NUTRITION FACTS

Calories: 290 | Carbohydrates: 20.9g | Fat: 1.9g | Protein: 37.3g | Cholesterol: 72mg | Sodium: 846mg

INGREDIENTS

- 3 tablespoons white miso paste
- 2 tablespoons water
- 2 tablespoons mirin (Japanese sweet wine)
- 2 tablespoons sake
- 1 tablespoon brown sugar
- 2 (7 ounce) black cod fillets

DIRECTIONS

1. Set oven rack about 6 inches from the heat source and preheat the oven's broiler. Line a baking sheet with aluminum foil and lightly grease the aluminum foil.
2. Whisk miso paste, water, mirin, sake, and brown sugar together in a small skillet over medium heat until mixture simmers and thickens slightly, 1 to 3 minutes. Remove from heat and cool completely.
3. Place cod fillets on prepared baking sheet. Brush fillets all over with miso mixture. Rest fillets at room temperature to quickly marinate, 15 to 20.
4. Broil fillets in the preheated oven for 5 minutes. Turn the baking sheet 180 degrees and continue broiling until fish flakes easily with a fork, about 5 minutes more. Remove pin bones.

MUSHROOM SPINACH OMELET

Servings: 2 | Prep: 15m | Cooks: 15m | Total: 30m

NUTRITION FACTS

Calories: 164.5 | Carbohydrates: 2.8g | Protein: 18.1g | Cholesterol: 7.8mg | Sodium: 584.4mg

INGREDIENTS

- 1 (8 ounce) carton liquid egg substitute
- 1 tablespoon shredded Cheddar cheese
- 1 tablespoon shredded Parmesan cheese
- 1/4 teaspoon salt
- 1/8 teaspoon ground black pepper
- 1/8 teaspoon garlic powder
- 1/8 teaspoon red pepper flakes
- 1 teaspoon olive oil
- 1/2 cup chopped fresh mushrooms
- 1 tablespoon chopped onion
- 1/2 cup chopped fresh spinach, or more to taste

DIRECTIONS

1. Whisk egg substitute, Cheddar cheese, Parmesan cheese, salt, black pepper, garlic powder, and red pepper flakes together in a bowl.
2. Heat olive oil in a nonstick skillet over medium heat; cook and stir mushrooms and onion until tender, 4 to 5 minutes. Add spinach; cook until spinach wilts, 3 to 4 minutes. Pour in egg mixture; swirl pan around to evenly distribute egg mixture. Cook until egg is fully cooked and set in the middle, 5 to 10 minutes. Cut into wedges.

CRAB-STUFFED LOBSTER TAIL

Servings: 2 | Prep: 20m | Cooks: 10m | Total: 30m

NUTRITION FACTS

Calories: 596.2 | Carbohydrates: 19.4g | Protein: 35.9g | Cholesterol: 203.3mg | Sodium: 1483.3mg

INGREDIENTS

- 2 large (blank)s lobster tails, split along the center top
- 2 teaspoons butter, melted
- 1 teaspoon seafood seasoning (such as Old Bay)
- 1 clove garlic, minced

- 15 eaches buttery round crackers, crushed
- 1/2 cup jumbo lump crabmeat
- 1/4 cup clarified butter
- 1 tablespoon chopped fresh parsley leaves
- 1 teaspoon lemon zest
- 1 tablespoon fresh lemon juice
- 1/4 teaspoon salt, or to taste
- 1/4 teaspoon freshly ground white pepper, or to taste

DIRECTIONS

1. Preheat oven to 425 degrees F (220 degrees C).
2. Pull the edges of the split lobster shells apart and gently lift the tail meat to rest above the shells. Place the prepared lobster tails on a baking sheet.
3. Brush each portion of tail meat with 1 teaspoon melted butter.
4. Lightly mix the crushed crackers, crabmeat, 1/4 cup of clarified butter, parsley, seafood seasoning, garlic, lemon zest, lemon juice, salt, and white pepper in a bowl until thoroughly combined.
5. Spoon half the stuffing onto each lobster tail; press lightly to slightly shape the stuffing so it doesn't fall off.
6. Bake the lobster tails in the preheated oven until the meat is opaque and the stuffing is golden brown on top, 10 to 12 minutes. An instant-read thermometer inserted into the thickest part of the lobster tail should read 145 degrees F (65 degrees C).

BROWN RICE BREAKFAST PORRIDGE

Servings: 2 | Prep: 5m | Cooks: 25m | Total: 30m

NUTRITION FACTS

Calories: 318.3 | Carbohydrates: 44.7g | Protein: 9.9g | Cholesterol: 118mg | Sodium: 130.3mg

INGREDIENTS

- 1 cup cooked brown rice
- 1 cup 2% low-fat milk
- 2 tablespoons dried blueberries
- 1 dash cinnamon
- 1 tablespoon honey
- 1 egg
- 1/4 teaspoon vanilla extract
- 1 tablespoon butter

DIRECTIONS

1. Combine the cooked brown rice, milk, blueberries, cinnamon, and honey in a small saucepan. Bring to a boil, then reduce heat to low and simmer for 20 minutes.
2. Beat the egg in a small bowl. Temper the egg by whisking in some of the hot rice, a tablespoon at a time until you have incorporated about 6 tablespoons. Stir the egg into the rice along with the vanilla and butter, and continue cooking over low heat for 1 to 2 minutes to thicken.

BAKED SALMON

Servings: 2 | Prep: 15m | Cooks: 45m | Total: 2h | Additional: 1h

NUTRITION FACTS

Calories: 612.5 | Carbohydrates: 2.9g | Protein: 36.3g | Cholesterol: 74.7mg | Sodium: 1234.5mg

INGREDIENTS

- 2 cloves garlic, minced
- 6 tablespoons light olive oil
- 1 teaspoon dried basil
- 1 teaspoon salt
- 1 teaspoon ground black pepper
- 1 tablespoon lemon juice
- 1 tablespoon fresh parsley, chopped
- 2 (6 ounce) fillets salmon

DIRECTIONS

1. In a medium glass bowl, prepare marinade by mixing garlic, light olive oil, basil, salt, pepper, lemon juice and parsley. Place salmon fillets in a medium glass baking dish, and cover with the marinade. Marinate in the refrigerator about 1 hour, turning occasionally.
2. Preheat oven to 375 degrees F (190 degrees C).
3. Place fillets in aluminum foil, cover with marinade, and seal. Place sealed salmon in the glass dish, and bake 35 to 45 minutes, until easily flaked with a fork.

CREAMY CAJUN CHICKEN PASTA

Servings: 2 | Prep: 15m | Cooks: 15m | Total: 30m

NUTRITION FACTS

Calories: 1109.2 | Carbohydrates: 53.7g | Protein: 42.7g | Cholesterol: 347.9mg | Sodium: 1134.2mg

INGREDIENTS

- 4 ounces linguine pasta
- 2 boneless, skinless chicken breast halves, sliced into thin strips
- 2 teaspoons Cajun seasoning
- 2 tablespoons butter
- 1 green bell pepper, chopped
- 1/2 red bell pepper, chopped
- 4 fresh mushrooms, sliced
- 1 green onion, minced
- 1 1/2 cups heavy cream
- 1/4 teaspoon dried basil
- 1/4 teaspoon lemon pepper
- 1/4 teaspoon salt
- 1/8 teaspoon garlic powder
- 1/8 teaspoon ground black pepper
- 2 tablespoons grated Parmesan cheese

DIRECTIONS

1. Bring a large pot of lightly salted water to a boil. Add linguini pasta, and cook for 8 to 10 minutes, or until al dente; drain.
2. Meanwhile, place chicken and Cajun seasoning in a bowl, and toss to coat.
3. In a large skillet over medium heat, saute chicken in butter until no longer pink and juices run clear, about 5 to 7 minutes. Add green and red bell peppers, sliced mushrooms and green onions; cook for 2 to 3 minutes. Reduce heat, and stir in heavy cream. Season the sauce with basil, lemon pepper, salt, garlic powder and ground black pepper, and heat through.
4. In a large bowl, toss linguini with sauce. Sprinkle with grated Parmesan cheese.

CAJUN CHICKEN PASTA

Servings: 2 | Prep: 20m | Cooks: 20m | Total: 40m

NUTRITION FACTS

Calories: 934.6 | Carbohydrates: 54g | Protein: 43.7g | Cholesterol: 270.8mg | Sodium: 1189.2mg

INGREDIENTS

- 4 ounces linguine pasta
- 2 skinless, boneless chicken breast halves
- 2 teaspoons Cajun seasoning
- 1 cup heavy cream
- 1/4 teaspoon dried basil
- 1/4 teaspoon lemon pepper

- 2 tablespoons butter
- 1 red bell pepper, sliced
- 1 green bell pepper, sliced
- 4 fresh mushrooms, sliced
- 1 green onion, chopped
- 1/4 teaspoon salt
- 1/8 teaspoon garlic powder
- 1/8 teaspoon ground black pepper
- 1/4 cup grated Parmesan cheese

DIRECTIONS

1. Bring a large pot of lightly salted water to a boil. Add pasta and cook for 8 to 10 minutes or until al dente; drain.
2. Place the chicken and the Cajun seasoning in a plastic bag. Shake to coat. In a large skillet over medium heat, saute the chicken in butter or margarine until almost tender (5 to 7 minutes).
3. Add the red bell pepper, green bell pepper, mushrooms and green onion. Saute and stir for 2 to 3 minutes. Reduce heat.
4. Add the cream, basil, lemon pepper, salt, garlic powder and ground black pepper. Heat through. Add the cooked linguine, toss and heat through. Sprinkle with grated Parmesan cheese and serve.

DELICIOUS BLACK BEAN BURRITOS

Servings: 2 | Prep: 10m | Cooks: 15m | Total: 25m

NUTRITION FACTS

Calories: 692 | Carbohydrates: 70.2g | Fat: 35.8g | Protein: 21.2g | Cholesterol: 47mg | Sodium: 1803mg

INGREDIENTS

- 2 (10 inch) flour tortillas
- 2 tablespoons vegetable oil
- 1 small onion, chopped
- 1/2 red bell pepper, chopped
- 1 teaspoon minced garlic
- 1 (15 ounce) can black beans, rinsed and drained
- 1 teaspoon minced jalapeno peppers
- 3 ounces cream cheese
- 1/2 teaspoon salt
- 2 tablespoons chopped fresh cilantro

DIRECTIONS

1. Wrap tortillas in foil and place in oven heated to 350 degrees F (175 degrees C). Bake for 15 minutes or until heated through.
2. Heat oil in a 10-inch skillet over medium heat. Place onion, bell pepper, garlic and jalapenos in skillet, cook for 2 minutes stirring occasionally. Pour beans into skillet, cook 3 minutes stirring.
3. Cut cream cheese into cubes and add to skillet with salt. Cook for 2 minutes stirring occasionally. Stir cilantro into mixture.
4. Spoon mixture evenly down center of warmed tortilla and roll tortillas up. Serve immediately.

CHICKEN PARMIGIANA

Servings: 2 | Prep: 30m | Cooks: 1h | Total: 1h30m

NUTRITION FACTS

Calories: 528.3 | Carbohydrates: 44.9g | Protein: 43.5g | Cholesterol: 184.1mg | Sodium: 1309.5mg

INGREDIENTS

- 1 egg, beaten
- 2 ounces dry bread crumbs
- 2 skinless, boneless chicken breast halves
- 3/4 (16 ounce) jar spaghetti sauce
- 2 ounces shredded mozzarella cheese
- 1/4 cup grated Parmesan cheese

DIRECTIONS

1. Preheat oven to 350 degrees F (175 degrees C). Lightly grease a medium baking sheet.
2. Pour egg into a small shallow bowl. Place bread crumbs in a separate shallow bowl. Dip chicken into egg, then into the bread crumbs. Place coated chicken on the prepared baking sheet and bake in the preheated oven for 40 minutes, or until no longer pink and juices run clear.
3. Pour 1/2 of the spaghetti sauce into a 7x11 inch baking dish. Place chicken over sauce, and cover with remaining sauce. Sprinkle mozzarella and Parmesan cheeses on top and return to the preheated oven for 20 minutes.

FILET MIGNON WITH RICH BALSAMIC GLAZE

Servings: 2 | Prep: 5m | Cooks: 15m | Total: 20m

NUTRITION FACTS

Calories: 366.6 | Carbohydrates: 5.7g | Protein: 20.3g | Cholesterol: 80.5mg | Sodium: 63.5mg

INGREDIENTS

- 2 (4 ounce) filet mignon steaks
- 1/2 teaspoon freshly ground black pepper to taste
- salt to taste
- 1/4 cup balsamic vinegar
- 1/4 cup dry red wine

DIRECTIONS

1. Sprinkle freshly ground pepper over both sides of each steak, and sprinkle with salt to taste.
2. Heat a nonstick skillet over medium-high heat. Place steaks in hot pan, and cook for 1 minute on each side, or until browned. Reduce heat to medium-low, and add balsamic vinegar and red wine. Cover, and cook for 4 minutes on each side, basting with sauce when you turn the meat over.
3. Remove steaks to two warmed plates, spoon one tablespoon of glaze over each, and serve immediately.

SAVORY GARLIC MARINATED STEAKS

Servings: 2 | Prep: 15m | Cooks: 15m | Total: 1d | Additional: 1d

NUTRITION FACTS

Calories: 576.4 | Carbohydrates: 36g | Protein: 28.4g | Cholesterol: 81.2mg | Sodium: 2496.5mg

INGREDIENTS

- 1/2 cup balsamic vinegar
- 1/4 cup soy sauce
- 3 tablespoons minced garlic
- 2 tablespoons honey
- 2 tablespoons olive oil
- 2 teaspoons ground black pepper
- 1 teaspoon Worcestershire sauce
- 1 teaspoon onion powder
- 1/2 teaspoon salt
- 1/2 teaspoon liquid smoke flavoring
- 1 pinch cayenne pepper
- 2 (1/2 pound) rib-eye steaks

DIRECTIONS

1. In a medium bowl, mix the vinegar, soy sauce, garlic, honey, olive oil, ground black pepper, Worcestershire sauce, onion powder, salt, liquid smoke, and cayenne pepper.

2. Place steaks in a shallow glass dish with the marinade, and turn to coat. For optimum flavor, rub the liquid into the meat. Cover, and marinate in the refrigerator for 1 to 2 days.
3. Preheat grill for medium-high to high heat.
4. Lightly oil the grill grate. Grill steaks 7 minutes per side, or to desired doneness. Discard leftover marinade.

STUFFED PEPPERS MY WAY

Servings: 2 | Prep: 20m | Cooks: 40m | Total: 1h

NUTRITION FACTS

Calories: 384.8 | Carbohydrates: 52.6g | Protein: 10.8g | Cholesterol: 33.4mg | Sodium: 159.5mg

INGREDIENTS

- 1 cup water
- 1/2 cup uncooked Arborio rice
- 2 green bell peppers, halved and seeded
- 1 tablespoon olive oil
- 2 green onions, thinly sliced
- 1 teaspoon dried basil
- 1 teaspoon Italian seasoning
- 1 teaspoon salt
- 1 pinch ground black pepper
- 1 tomato, diced
- 1/2 cup crumbled feta cheese

DIRECTIONS

1. Preheat oven to 400 degrees F (200 degrees C). Lightly grease a baking sheet.
2. In a medium saucepan, bring water to a boil. Stir in the rice. Reduce heat, cover, and simmer for 20 minutes. Remove from heat, and set aside.
3. Place the peppers cut-side down on the prepared baking sheet. Roast 25 to 30 minutes in the preheated oven, or until tender and skin starts to brown.
4. While the peppers are roasting, heat oil in a medium skillet over medium-high heat. Cook the onions, basil, Italian seasoning, salt, and pepper in oil for 2 to 3 minutes. Stir in the tomato, and cook for 5 minutes. Spoon in the cooked rice, and stir until heated through. Remove from heat, mix in the feta cheese, and spoon the mixture into the pepper halves.
5. Return to the oven for 5 minutes. Serve immediately.

CHICKEN MARSALA

Servings: 2 | Prep: 20m | Cooks: 40m | Total: 1h

NUTRITION FACTS

Calories: 789.7 | Carbohydrates: 26.8g | Protein: 51.1g | Cholesterol: 185.4mg | Sodium: 2390.8mg

INGREDIENTS

- 2 eaches skin-on, boneless chicken breast halves
- 1 teaspoon salt and ground black pepper to taste
- 3 tablespoons butter, divided
- 2 tablespoons olive oil
- 5 white mushrooms, sliced
- 1 shallot, minced
- 1 tablespoon all-purpose flour
- 1 cup Marsala wine
- 2 cups chicken stock
- 2 tablespoons chopped fresh parsley
- 1 teaspoon cold butter

DIRECTIONS

1. Season chicken breasts all over with salt and pepper.
2. Melt 1 1/2 tablespoons butter and olive oil in a skillet over medium heat. Cook chicken breasts, skin-side down, in hot butter and oil until browned, about 5 minutes. Flip and cook until breasts are almost cooked through, about 5 minutes more. Transfer chicken breasts to a plate.
3. Melt 1 1/2 tablespoons butter in the same skillet over medium-high heat. Saute mushrooms with a pinch of salt and a pinch of pepper in hot butter until mushrooms are golden, 5 to 7 minutes. Add minced shallot; cook and stir until softened, 2 to 3 minutes. Sprinkle flour over the top and cook and stir until the bitterness of the flour cooks off, 3 to 4 minutes.
4. Pour wine into skillet and bring to a boil; cook and stir until wine reduces and sauce thickens, 3 to 4 minutes. Add chicken stock; bring to a simmer and cook until slightly reduced, 3 to 5 minutes more.
5. Return chicken breasts to the skillet, reduce heat to low, and cook chicken, turning once, until no longer pink in the center and the juices run clear, about 10 minutes. An instant-read thermometer inserted into the center should read at least 165 degrees F (74 degrees C). Remove from heat.
6. Move chicken to one side of the skillet and tilt the skillet so that the sauce pools at the bottom. Stir parsley and 1 teaspoon cold butter into the sauce, stirring constantly, until sauce is shiny and butter is completely melted. Transfer chicken breasts to plates and spoon mushrooms and sauce over the top.

OVEN BBQ CHICKEN DRUMSTICKS

Servings: 3 | Prep: 10m | Cooks: 1h | Total: 1h10m

NUTRITION FACTS

Calories: 443.3 | Carbohydrates: 20.7g| Protein: 39.4g | Cholesterol: 142.3mg | Sodium: 2071.9mg

INGREDIENTS

- 6 chicken drumsticks
- 1/2 cup water
- 1/3 cup ketchup
- 1/3 cup white vinegar
- 1/4 cup brown sugar
- 4 teaspoons butter
- 2 teaspoons salt
- 2 teaspoons Worcestershire sauce, or to taste
- 2 teaspoons dry mustard
- 2 teaspoons chili powder, or to taste

DIRECTIONS

1. Preheat oven to 400 degrees F (200 degrees C). Place drumsticks in a baking dish.
2. Whisk water, ketchup, vinegar, brown sugar, butter, salt, Worcestershire sauce, mustard, and chili powder together in a bowl; pour mixture over drumsticks. Cover with aluminum foil
3. Bake in preheated oven until no longer pink at the bone and the juices run clear, about 1 hour, turning chicken about halfway through. An instant-read thermometer inserted near the bone should read 165 degrees F (74 degrees C).

MAMA'S BEST BROILED TOMATO SANDWICH

Servings: 2 | Prep: 10m | Cooks: 5m | Total: 15m

NUTRITION FACTS

Calories: 509.2 | Carbohydrates: 43.2g | Protein: 9.6g | Cholesterol: 14.5mg | Sodium: 605.2mg

INGREDIENTS

- 2 tablespoons olive oil
- 2 tablespoons balsamic vinegar
- 4 ripe tomatoes, sliced
- 1/4 teaspoon dried oregano
- 1/4 teaspoon black pepper
- 3 tablespoons grated Parmesan cheese, divided

- 3 tablespoons mayonnaise
- 1/2 teaspoon dried parsley
- 4 slices bread, lightly toasted

DIRECTIONS

1. Preheat oven to broil.
2. In a shallow bowl, whisk together the olive oil and vinegar. Marinate the tomatoes in the mixture, stirring occasionally.
3. Meanwhile, in a small bowl, combine mayonnaise, parsley, oregano, black pepper and 4 teaspoons Parmesan cheese. Spread mixture on each slice of toasted bread. Place marinated tomatoes on 2 slices and sprinkle with remaining Parmesan cheese.
4. Place on a baking sheet and broil for 5 minutes, or until cheese turns golden brown. Serve immediately, open faced or closed.

PEANUT NOODLES

Servings: 3 | Prep: 10m | Cooks: 15m | Total: 25m

NUTRITION FACTS

Calories: 568 | Carbohydrates: 70.1g | Fat: 24.8g | Protein: 19.7g | Cholesterol: 0mg | Sodium: 1352mg

INGREDIENTS

- 8 ounces spaghetti
- 1 bunch green onions, sliced (white parts only)
- 2 tablespoons sesame oil
- 1 teaspoon minced fresh ginger root
- 1/3 cup peanut butter
- 1/4 cup soy sauce
- 1/4 cup hot water
- 1 tablespoon cider vinegar
- 1 teaspoon white sugar
- 1/4 teaspoon crushed red pepper flakes

DIRECTIONS

1. Cook pasta in a large pot of boiling water until done. Drain.
2. Meanwhile, combine oil and onions in a small skillet. Saute over low heat until tender. Add ginger; cook and stir for 1 to 2 minutes. Mix in peanut butter, soy sauce, water, vinegar, sugar, and red pepper flakes. Remove from heat.
3. Toss noodles with sauce, and serve.

GRILLED FISH STEAKS

Servings: 2 | Prep: 10m | Cooks: 10m | Total: 1h30m | Additional: 1h10m

NUTRITION FACTS

Calories: 554.3 | Carbohydrates: 2.2g | Protein: 36.3g | Cholesterol: 62.5mg | Sodium: 1259.3mg

INGREDIENTS

- 1 clove garlic, minced
- 6 tablespoons olive oil
- 1 teaspoon dried basil
- 1 teaspoon salt
- 1 teaspoon ground black pepper
- 1 tablespoon fresh lemon juice
- 1 tablespoon chopped fresh parsley
- 2 (6 ounce) fillets halibut

DIRECTIONS

1. In a stainless steel or glass bowl, combine garlic, olive oil, basil, salt, pepper, lemon juice, and parsley.
2. Place the halibut filets in a shallow glass dish or a resealable plastic bag, and pour the marinade over the fish. Cover or seal and place in the refrigerator for 1 hour, turning occasionally.
3. Preheat an outdoor grill for high heat and lightly oil grate. Set grate 4 inches from the heat.
4. Remove halibut filets from marinade and drain off the excess. Grill filets 5 minutes per side or until fish is done when easily flaked with a fork.

ASPARAGUS AND MOZZARELLA STUFFED CHICKEN BREASTS

Servings: 2 | Prep: 20m | Cooks: 25m | Total: 45m

NUTRITION FACTS

Calories: 390.4 | Carbohydrates: 13.3g | Protein: 57.4g | Cholesterol: 147.3mg | Sodium: 581.1mg

INGREDIENTS

- 2 large skinless, boneless chicken breast halves
- 1 pinch salt and black pepper to taste
- 8 asparagus spears, trimmed - divided
- 1/2 cup shredded mozzarella cheese, divided
- 1/4 cup Italian seasoned bread crumbs

DIRECTIONS

1. Preheat an oven to 375 degrees F (190 degrees C). Grease an 8x8-inch baking dish.
2. Place each chicken breast between two sheets of heavy plastic (resealable freezer bags work well) on a solid, level surface. Firmly pound the chicken with the smooth side of a meat mallet to an even thickness of about 1/4 inch. Sprinkle each side with salt and pepper.
3. Place 4 spears of asparagus down the center of a chicken breast, and spread about 1/4 cup of mozzarella cheese over the asparagus. Repeat with the other chicken breast, and roll the chicken around the asparagus and cheese to make a tidy, compact roll. Place the rolls seam sides down in the prepared baking dish, and sprinkle each with about 2 tablespoons of bread crumbs.
4. Bake in the preheated oven until the juices run clear when pricked with a fork, about 25 minutes. An instant-read thermometer inserted into the center should read at least 165 degrees F (74 degrees C).

CHICKEN SCARPARIELLO

Servings: 2 | Prep: 15m | Cooks: 20m | Total: 35m

NUTRITION FACTS

Calories: 580.1 | Carbohydrates: 14.3g | Protein: 67.7g | Cholesterol: 175.8mg | Sodium: 1085.8mg

INGREDIENTS

- 1 1/4 pounds skinless, boneless chicken breast halves
- 3 tablespoons all-purpose flour
- 2 tablespoons olive oil
- 2 teaspoons butter
- 2 tablespoons shallots, minced
- 2 cloves garlic, minced
- 1 cup water
- 1/2 cup white wine
- 1 cube chicken bouillon
- 1/2 teaspoon dried rosemary, crushed
- 1/4 teaspoon salt
- 1 pinch ground black pepper

DIRECTIONS

1. Cut chicken breasts into 1 x 3 inch strips, and dredge in flour.
2. In 10 inch skillet, heat oil and butter. Add chicken. Cook, turning occasionally, until lightly browned on all sides (3 to 4 minutes). Using tongs, remove chicken from skillet. Set aside and keep warm.
3. To same skillet, add shallots and garlic. Saute until softened (1 minute). Add water, wine, broth mix, and seasonings. Mix well. Cook, stirring frequently, until liquid is reduced by 1/2 (3 to 4 minutes). Return chicken to skillet, and cook until sauce is thick and chicken is heated through (2 to 3 minutes).

QUICK GNOCCHI

Servings: 2 | Prep: 10m | Cooks: 5m | Total: 15m

NUTRITION FACTS

Calories: 462.3 | Carbohydrates: 91.3g | Protein: 14.8g | Cholesterol: 93mg | Sodium: 124.6mg

INGREDIENTS

- 1 cup dry potato flakes
- 1 cup boiling water
- 1 egg, beaten
- 1 teaspoon salt
- 1/8 teaspoon ground black pepper
- 1 1/2 cups all-purpose flour

DIRECTIONS

1. Place potato flakes in a medium-size bowl. Pour in boiling water; stir until blended. Let cool.
2. Stir in egg, salt, and pepper. Blend in enough flour to make a fairly stiff dough. Turn dough out on a well floured board. Knead lightly.
3. Divide dough in half. Shape each half into a long thin roll, the thickness of a breadstick. With a knife dipped in flour, cut into bite-size pieces.
4. Place a few gnocchi in boiling water. As the gnocchi rise to the top of the pot, remove them with a slotted spoon. Repeat until all are cooked.

BAKED SPLIT CHICKEN BREAST

Servings: 2 | Prep: 10m | Cooks: 45m | Total: 1h40m | Additional: 45m

NUTRITION FACTS

Calories: 614.7 | Carbohydrates: 0.7g | Protein: 54.5g | Cholesterol: 153.3mg | Sodium: 570mg

INGREDIENTS

- 2 large (blank)s large bone-in chicken breast halves with skin
- 1/4 cup extra-virgin olive oil
- 1/2 teaspoon garlic, minced
- 1/2 teaspoon coarse sea salt
- 1/2 teaspoon cracked black pepper
- 1/4 teaspoon dried rosemary
- 1/4 teaspoon dried basil

DIRECTIONS

1. Rub chicken breasts with olive oil and garlic; sprinkle with salt, black pepper, rosemary, and basil. Arrange chicken in a large baking dish and refrigerate at least 45 minutes.
2. Preheat oven to 375 degrees F (190 degrees C).
3. Bake in preheated oven until chicken meat is no longer pink at the bone and the juices run clear, 45 to 60 minutes. An instant-read thermometer inserted in the thickest part of the breast meat should read 165 degrees F (75 degrees C).

GRILLED ROCK LOBSTER TAILS

Servings: 2 | Prep: 15m | Cooks: 12m | Total: 27m

NUTRITION FACTS

Calories: 742.2 | Carbohydrates: 4.3g | Protein: 44.3g | Cholesterol: 169.3mg | Sodium: 2036mg

INGREDIENTS

- 1 tablespoon lemon juice
- 1/2 cup olive oil
- 1 teaspoon salt
- 1 teaspoon paprika
- 1/8 teaspoon white pepper
- 1/8 teaspoon garlic powder
- 2 (10 ounce) rock lobster tails

DIRECTIONS

1. Preheat grill for high heat.
2. Squeeze lemon juice into a small bowl, and slowly whisk in olive oil. Whisk in salt, paprika, white pepper, and garlic powder. Split lobster tails lengthwise with a large knife, and brush flesh side of tail with marinade.
3. Lightly oil grill grate. Place tails, flesh side down, on preheated grill. Cook for 10 to 12 minutes, turning once, and basting frequently with marinade. Discard any remaining marinade. Lobster is done when opaque and firm to the touch.

EASY MARINATED PORK TENDERLOIN

Servings: 3 | Prep: 10m | Cooks: 45m | Total: 1h55m | Additional: 1h

NUTRITION FACTS

Calories: 485.4 | Carbohydrates: 9g | Protein: 55.5g | Cholesterol: 168.7mg | Sodium: 1491.8mg

INGREDIENTS

- 1/4 cup olive oil
- 1/4 cup soy sauce
- 1 clove garlic, minced
- 3 tablespoons dijon honey mustard
- 1 pinch salt and ground black pepper to taste
- 2 pounds pork tenderloin

DIRECTIONS

1. Whisk together the olive oil, soy sauce, garlic, mustard, salt, and pepper in a bowl. Place the pork loin in a large resealable plastic bag and pour in the marinade. Marinate in the refrigerator at least 1 hour before cooking.
2. Preheat an oven to 350 degrees F (175 degrees C).
3. Transfer the pork loin to a baking dish; pour marinade over the pork.
4. Cook in the preheated oven until the pork is no longer pink in the center, 45 to 60 minutes. An instant-read thermometer inserted into the center should read 145 degrees F (63 degrees C).

PORK TENDERLOIN DIABLO

Servings: 3 | Prep: 5m | Cooks: 30m | Total: 40m | Additional: 5m

NUTRITION FACTS

Calories: 235 | Carbohydrates: 2g | Fat: 14.1g | Protein: 23.7g | Cholesterol: 89mg | Sodium: 223mg

INGREDIENTS

- 1 (1 pound) whole pork tenderloin
- salt and freshly ground black pepper to taste
- 2 teaspoons vegetable oil
- 1/2 cup chicken broth
- 2 tablespoons heavy cream
- 1 tablespoon extra-hot prepared horseradish
- 1 tablespoon Dijon mustard
- 1/4 teaspoon cayenne pepper
- 1 tablespoon cold butter
- 1 teaspoon chopped fresh chives

DIRECTIONS

1. Preheat oven to 375 degrees F (190 degrees C). Season pork with salt and pepper.
2. Heat oil in an ovenproof skillet over high heat. Cook pork until browned on one side, 3 to 4 minutes. Turn over pork and transfer the skillet to the preheated oven. Cook until pork is browned and still

slightly pink in the center, 20 to 25 minutes. An instant-read thermometer inserted into the center should read at least 145 degrees F (63 degrees C). Transfer pork to a plate.

3. Remove any excess oil from the skillet and place it over medium-high heat. Pour in chicken broth and bring to a boil, scraping any browned bits off of the bottom of the pan. Whisk in cream, horseradish, Dijon mustard, and cayenne pepper. Continue cooking until the mixture is reduced to a thick sauce, 3 to 4 minutes. Remove from heat and whisk in cold butter. Stir in chives.

4. Slice pork into 1/2-inch slices and serve topped with sauce.

BROILED SCALLOPS

Servings: 3 | Prep: 5m | Cooks: 8m | Total: 13m

NUTRITION FACTS

Calories: 272.9 | Carbohydrates: 6.8g | Protein: 38.3g | Cholesterol: 95.3mg | Sodium: 2232.2mg

INGREDIENTS

- 1 1/2 pounds bay scallops
- 2 tablespoons butter, melted
- 1 tablespoon garlic salt
- 2 tablespoons lemon juice

DIRECTIONS

1. Turn broiler on.
2. Rinse scallop and place in a shallow baking pan. Sprinkle with garlic salt, melted butter or margarine and lemon juice.
3. Broil 6 to 8 minutes or until scallops start to turn golden. Remove from oven and serve with extra melted butter or margarine on the side for dipping.

GRILLED PORK LOIN CHOPS

Servings: 2 | Prep: 10m | Cooks: 25m | Total: 4h35m| Additional: 4h

NUTRITION FACTS

Calories: 429 | Carbohydrates: 49.3g | Protein: 39.5g | Cholesterol: 97.9mg | Sodium: 1725.7mg

INGREDIENTS

- 2 cloves garlic, minced
- 2 tablespoons brown sugar
- 1/2 teaspoon ground ginger
- 1/2 teaspoon onion powder

- 3 tablespoons honey
- 3 tablespoons soy sauce
- 3 tablespoons Worcestershire sauce
- 2 teaspoons ketchup
- 1/4 teaspoon ground cinnamon
- 1/8 teaspoon cayenne pepper
- 2 (6 ounce) thick-cut boneless pork loin chops

DIRECTIONS

1. Mix the garlic, brown sugar, honey, soy sauce, Worcestershire sauce, ketchup, ginger, onion powder, cinnamon, and cayenne pepper together in a bowl. Pour half the mixture into a large plastic zipper bag, and place the pork chops into the marinade. Squeeze the air out of the bag, and seal the bag. Refrigerate 4 to 8 hours, turning occasionally. Refrigerate remaining marinade in the bowl.
2. Preheat an outdoor grill for medium heat, and lightly oil the grate.
3. Remove the pork chops from the plastic bag, and shake excess droplets of liquid from the chops. Discard the marinade from the plastic bag. Grill chops on the preheated grill, basting with the reserved marinade until meat is browned, no longer pink inside, and shows good grill marks, 8 to 10 minutes per side. A meat thermometer inserted into the thickest part of a chop should read at least 145 degrees F (63 degrees C).
4. Pour remaining reserved marinade into a saucepan over medium heat, bring to a boil, and reduce heat to a simmer. Cook the marinade until slightly thickened, about 5 minutes, stirring constantly; serve sauce with chops.

BROCCOLI AND CHICKEN STIR-FRY

Servings: 3 | Prep: 15m | Cooks: 20m | Total: 35m

NUTRITION FACTS

Calories: 356.1 | Carbohydrates: 40.7g | Protein: 33.4g | Cholesterol: 71.9mg | Sodium: 3307.3mg

INGREDIENTS

- 2/3 cup soy sauce
- 1/4 cup brown sugar
- 1/2 teaspoon ground ginger
- 1 pinch red pepper flakes, or to taste
- 2 tablespoons water
- 2 tablespoons cornstarch
- 2 teaspoons vegetable oil, or to taste
- 3 skinless, boneless chicken breast halves, cut into chunks
- 1 onion, sliced
- 3 cups broccoli florets

DIRECTIONS

1. Stir soy sauce, brown sugar, ginger, and red pepper flakes together in a bowl to dissolve sugar into the liquid. Mix water and cornstarch together in a small bowl; stir with a whisk until cornstarch dissolves completely.
2. Heat oil in a large skillet over high heat. Fry chicken and onion in hot oil until the chicken is no longer pink in the center and the onion is tender, 5 to 7 minutes. Stir broccoli with the chicken and onion; saute until the broccoli is hot, about 5 minutes. Push the chicken and vegetables mixture to the side of the skillet.
3. Pour the soy sauce mixture into the vacant part of the skillet. Stir the cornstarch slurry into the soy sauce mixture until the color is consistent. Move the chicken and vegetables back into the center to the pan; saute until the sauce thickens and coats the chicken and vegetables, about 5 minutes more.

CHICKEN AND MUSHROOMS

Servings: 2 | Prep: 10m | Cooks: 30m | Total: 40m

NUTRITION FACTS

Calories: 397.8 | Carbohydrates: 3.7g | Protein: 28.1g | Cholesterol: 90.8mg | Sodium: 355.4mg

INGREDIENTS

- 2 chicken breast halves, boneless, skin-on
- 1 pinch salt and ground black pepper to taste
- 2 tablespoons olive oil
- 8 ounces fresh mushrooms, sliced 1/4 inch thick
- 1 pinch salt
- 1/2 cup water
- 1 tablespoon butter
- 1 pinch salt and ground black pepper to taste

DIRECTIONS

1. Preheat oven to 400 degrees F (200 degrees C).
2. Season chicken on all sides with salt and ground black pepper.
3. Heat olive oil over medium-high heat in an ovenproof skillet. Place chicken skin-side down in skillet and cook until browned, about 5 minutes.
4. Turn chicken over; stir mushrooms with a pinch of salt into skillet. Increase heat to high; cook, stirring mushrooms occasionally, until mushrooms shrink slightly, about 5 minutes.
5. Transfer skillet to the preheated oven and cook until chicken is no longer pink in the center and the juices run clear, 15 to 20 minutes. An instant-read thermometer inserted into the center should read 165 degrees F (74 degrees C). Transfer chicken breasts to a plate and loosely tent with foil; set aside.

6. Set skillet on the stovetop over medium-high heat; cook and stir mushrooms until brown bits start to form on the bottom of the pan, about 5 minutes. Pour water into the skillet, and bring to a boil while scraping the browned bits off of the bottom of the pan. Cook until water is reduced by half, about 2 minutes. Remove from heat.
7. Stir in any accumulated juices from the chicken into the skillet. Stir butter into mushroom mixture, stirring constantly until butter is completely melted and incorporated.
8. Season with salt and pepper. Spoon mushroom sauce over chicken and serve.

MARINATED RANCH BROILED CHICKEN

Servings: 2 | Prep: 5m | Cooks: 15m | Total: 1h20m | Additional: 1h

NUTRITION FACTS

Calories: 285.7 | Carbohydrates: 7.1g | Protein: 27.2g | Cholesterol: 68.4mg | | Sodium: 1057.3mg

INGREDIENTS

- 2 skinless, boneless chicken breast halves
- 2 tablespoons olive oil
- 1 (1 ounce) package dry Ranch-style dressing mix
- 1 tablespoon red wine vinegar

DIRECTIONS

1. Combine the dressing mix, oil and vinegar in a large, resealable plastic bag and mix together. Add chicken to bag, seal and shake to coat; work mixture into the meat.
2. Refrigerate to marinate for at least 1 hour, or overnight if possible.
3. Preheat oven to Broil/Grill.
4. Remove chicken from bag, discarding any remaining marinade, and broil for 10 to 15 minutes or until cooked through and no longer pink inside.

BROILED LOBSTER TAILS

Servings: 2 | Prep: 15m | Cooks: 5m | Total: 20m

NUTRITION FACTS

Calories: 591.8 | Carbohydrates: 7.4g | Protein: 37g | Cholesterol: 302.5mg | Sodium: 891.1mg

INGREDIENTS

- 2 whole lobster tails
- 1/2 cup butter, melted
- 1 pinch salt to taste
- 1 pinch ground white pepper, to taste

- 1/2 teaspoon ground paprika
- 1 lemon - cut into wedges, for garnish

DIRECTIONS

1. Preheat the broiler.
2. Place lobster tails on a baking sheet. With a sharp knife or kitchen shears, carefully cut top side of lobster shells lengthwise. Pull apart shells slightly, and season meat with equal amounts butter, paprika, salt, and white pepper.
3. Broil lobster tails until lightly browned and lobster meat is opaque, about 5 to 10 minutes. Garnish with lemon wedges to serve.

LEMON ROSEMARY SALMON

Servings: 2 | Prep: 10m | Cooks: 20m | Total: 30m

NUTRITION FACTS

Calories: 265.7 | Carbohydrates: 6.1g | Protein: 20.5g | Cholesterol: 56.4mg | Sodium: 1016.7mg

INGREDIENTS

- 1 lemon, thinly sliced
- 4 sprigs fresh rosemary
- 2 eaches salmon fillets, bones and skin removed
- 1 teaspoon coarse salt to taste
- 1 tablespoon olive oil, or as needed

DIRECTIONS

1. Preheat oven to 400 degrees F (200 degrees C).
2. Arrange half the lemon slices in a single layer in a baking dish. Layer with 2 sprigs rosemary, and top with salmon fillets. Sprinkle salmon with salt, layer with remaining rosemary sprigs, and top with remaining lemon slices. Drizzle with olive oil.
3. Bake 20 minutes in the preheated oven, or until fish is easily flaked with a fork.

PARMESAN SAGE PORK CHOPS

Servings: 2 | Prep: 30m | Cooks: 10m | Total: 40m

NUTRITION FACTS

Calories: 526.8 | Carbohydrates: 37.7g | Protein: 28.6g | Cholesterol: 155.6mg | Sodium: 1342.2mg

INGREDIENTS

- 2 tablespoons all-purpose flour
- 1/4 teaspoon salt
- 1 pinch ground black pepper
- 1 egg, lightly beaten
- 3/4 cup Italian bread crumbs
- 1/2 cup grated Parmesan cheese
- 1 1/2 teaspoons rubbed sage
- 1/2 teaspoon grated lemon zest
- 2 boneless pork chops
- 1 tablespoon olive oil
- 1 tablespoon butter

DIRECTIONS

1. Preheat oven to 425 degrees F (220 degrees C). Lightly grease a 7x11-inch baking dish.
2. Mix flour, salt, and ground pepper in a shallow dish. Combine bread crumbs, Parmesan cheese, sage, and lemon peel in a shallow dish. Gently press pork into flour mixture to coat and shake off excess flour. Dip into beaten egg, then press into bread crumbs. Gently toss between your hands so any bread crumbs that haven't stuck can fall away. Place breaded pork onto a plate while breading the rest; do not stack.
3. Heat olive oil and butter in a skillet over medium heat. Brown pork chops on each side, about 4 minutes per side, then transfer to baking dish.
4. Bake in preheated oven until juices run clear and a meat thermometer inserted into the middle of pork reads 160 degrees F (71 degrees C), 10 to 15 minutes.

BACON MUSHROOM CHICKEN

Servings: 2 | Prep: 15m | Cooks: 1h | Total: 1h15m

NUTRITION FACTS

Calories: 773.9 | Carbohydrates: 2.7g | Protein: 52.7g | Cholesterol: 241.1mg

INGREDIENTS

- 2 tablespoons butter, melted
- 2 bone-in chicken breast halves, with skin
- 1 teaspoon seasoning salt
- 1 clove garlic, crushed
- 2 thick slices bacon
- 1/2 cup mushrooms, halved
- 1/4 cup heavy cream

DIRECTIONS

1. Preheat oven to 350 degrees F (175 degrees C).
2. Pour melted butter into a 9x13 inch baking dish. Add chicken, skin side down; sprinkle with seasoning salt and garlic. Turn chicken over, season, and lay bacon strips on top. Sprinkle with mushrooms.
3. Bake in preheated oven for 45 minutes to 60 minutes, or until chicken is no longer pink and juices run clear.
4. Remove chicken, bacon and mushrooms to a platter and keep warm. Pour juices from baking dish into a small saucepan and whisk together with cream over low heat until thickened. Pour sauce over chicken and serve warm.

EMERGENCY CHICKEN

Servings: 2 | Prep: 5m | Cooks: 10m | Total: 15m

NUTRITION FACTS

Calories: 529.9 | Carbohydrates: 32.5g | Protein: 66.3g | Cholesterol: 190.8mg | Sodium: 1200.6mg

INGREDIENTS

- 1 tablespoon butter
- 2/3 cup barbeque sauce
- 1 tablespoon Worcestershire sauce
- 2/3 teaspoon garlic powder
- 1 1/2 pounds skinless, boneless chicken pieces

DIRECTIONS

1. Melt butter in a saucepan over medium heat. Stir barbeque sauce, Worcestershire sauce, and garlic powder together with the melted butter. Stir chicken into the sauce mixture to coat.
2. Place cover on saucepan and simmer until the chicken pieces are cooked through and no longer pink in the middle, 3 to 5 minutes. Remove cover and spoon sauce over chicken pieces; continue cooking until sauce thickens, about 4 minutes more.

FISH IN FOIL

Servings: 2 | Prep: 10m | Cooks: 20m | Total: 30m

NUTRITION FACTS

Calories: 213 | Carbohydrates: 7.5g | Fat: 10.9g | Protein: 24.3g | Cholesterol: 67mg | Sodium: 1850mg

INGREDIENTS

- 2 rainbow trout fillets
- 1 tablespoon olive oil
- 2 teaspoons garlic salt
- 1 teaspoon ground black pepper
- 1 fresh jalapeno pepper, sliced
- 1 lemon, sliced

DIRECTIONS

1. Preheat oven to 400 degrees F (200 degrees C). Rinse fish, and pat dry.
2. Rub fillets with olive oil, and season with garlic salt and black pepper. Place each fillet on a large sheet of aluminum foil. Top with jalapeno slices, and squeeze the juice from the ends of the lemons over the fish. Arrange lemon slices on top of fillets. Carefully seal all edges of the foil to form enclosed packets. Place packets on baking sheet.
3. Bake in preheated oven for 15 to 20 minutes, depending on the size of fish. Fish is done when it flakes easily with a fork.

CHICKEN WITH LEMON-CAPER SAUCE

Servings: 2 | Prep: 10m | Cooks: 20m | Total: 30m

NUTRITION FACTS

Calories: 661.9 | Carbohydrates: 29.2g | Protein: 43.3g | Cholesterol: 159.8mg | Sodium: 372mg

INGREDIENTS

- 1 pinch salt
- 1/2 cup all-purpose flour
- 2 (6 ounce) skinless, boneless chicken breast halves
- 2 tablespoons olive oil
- 1/4 cup dry white wine
- 1/4 cup lemon juice
- 1/4 cup cold unsalted butter, cut into pieces
- 2 tablespoons capers, drained
- 2 wedge (blank)s lemon wedges

DIRECTIONS

1. Mix together salt and flour in a small dish or plastic bag, then coat chicken and shake off excess. Heat olive oil in a skillet over medium-high heat. Shake excess flour from chicken, then brown in

hot oil until both sides are golden-brown, and the inside has turned white and firm, 3 to 4 minutes per side.

2. Remove the chicken, and set aside in a warm place. Pour white wine into the skillet, and allow to boil as you dissolve the cooked bits from the bottom of the pan. Add the lemon juice, and allow to come to a boil, cook for a few minutes until reduced by half.

3. Sprinkle the cubed butter into the boiling sauce. Swirl and shake the pan vigorously to dissolve the butter, thus thickening the sauce. The butter must never come to rest, or the sauce will separate and become oily. Once the butter has completely incorporated, remove from heat and stir in capers.

4. To serve, pour lemon-caper sauce over the chicken, and serve with a wedge of lemon.

ACAPULCO CHICKEN

Servings: 2 | Prep: 10m | Cooks: 15m | Total: 25m

NUTRITION FACTS

Calories: 332.5 | Carbohydrates: 23.8g | Protein: 30.1g | Cholesterol: 71.9mg | Sodium: 635.5mg

INGREDIENTS

- 2 skinless, boneless chicken breast halves - cut into bite-size pieces
- 1 tablespoon chili powder, divided
- salt and pepper to taste
- 1 tablespoon olive oil
- 1 cup chopped green bell pepper
- 1/2 cup chopped onion
- 2 jalapeno peppers, seeded and minced
- 1 large tomato, cut into chunks
- 10 drops hot pepper sauce

DIRECTIONS

1. Season chicken with 1/2 tablespoon chili powder, salt and pepper. Heat oil in a large skillet over medium high heat and saute seasoned chicken for 3 to 4 minutes, or until no longer pink. Remove from skillet with a slotted spoon and keep warm.

2. In same skillet, stir fry bell pepper and onion until soft. Add jalapeno peppers, tomatoes, remaining 1/2 tablespoon chili powder and hot pepper sauce. Cook, stirring, for an additional 3 to 5 minutes; add chicken and stir fry for 2 minutes more.

HONEY GRILLED SHRIMP

Servings: 3 | Prep: 30m | Cooks: 6m | Total: 1h36m | Additional: 1h

NUTRITION FACTS

Calories: 434.4 | Carbohydrates: 33.4g | Protein: 29.9g | Cholesterol: 279.5mg | Sodium: 1017.3mg

INGREDIENTS

- 1/2 teaspoon garlic powder
- 1/4 tablespoon ground black pepper
- 1/3 cup Worcestershire sauce
- 2 tablespoons dry white wine
- 2 tablespoons Italian-style salad dressing
- 1 pound large shrimp, peeled and deveined with tails attached
- 1/4 cup honey
- 1/4 cup butter, melted
- 2 tablespoons Worcestershire sauce
- 3 eaches skewers

DIRECTIONS

1. In a large bowl, mix together garlic powder, black pepper, 1/3 cup Worcestershire sauce, wine, and salad dressing; add shrimp, and toss to coat. Cover, and marinate in the refrigerator for 1 hour.
2. Preheat grill for high heat. Thread shrimp onto skewers, piercing once near the tail and once near the head. Discard marinade.
3. In a small bowl, stir together honey, melted butter, and remaining 2 tablespoons Worcestershire sauce. Set aside for basting.
4. Lightly oil grill grate. Grill shrimp for 2 to 3 minutes per side, or until opaque. Baste occasionally with the honey-butter sauce while grilling.

SPAGHETTI AGLIO E OLIO

Servings: 4 | Prep: 10m | Cooks: 22m | Total: 32m

NUTRITION FACTS

Calories: 755 | Carbohydrates: 87.4g | Fat: 34.5g | Protein: g | Cholesterol: 18mg | Sodium: 355mg

INGREDIENTS

- 1 pound uncooked spaghetti
- 6 cloves garlic, thinly sliced
- salt and freshly ground black pepper to taste
- 1/4 cup chopped fresh Italian parsley

- 1/2 cup olive oil

- 1/4 teaspoon red pepper flakes, or to taste

- 1 cup finely grated Parmigiano-Reggiano cheese

DIRECTIONS

1. Bring a large pot of lightly salted water to a boil. Cook spaghetti in the boiling water, stirring occasionally until cooked through but firm to the bite, about 12 minutes. Drain and transfer to a pasta bowl.
2. Combine garlic and olive oil in a cold skillet. Cook over medium heat to slowly toast garlic, about 10 minutes. Reduce heat to medium-low when olive oil begins to bubble. Cook and stir until garlic is golden brown, about another 5 minutes. Remove from heat.
3. Stir red pepper flakes, black pepper, and salt into the pasta. Pour in olive oil and garlic, and sprinkle on Italian parsley and half of the Parmigiano-Reggiano cheese; stir until combined.
4. Serve pasta topped with the remaining Parmigiano-Reggiano cheese.

SALMON WITH TOMATOES

Servings: 2 | Prep: 15m | Cooks: 30m | Total: 45m

NUTRITION FACTS

Calories: 955.5 | Carbohydrates: 85g | Protein: 41.9g | Cholesterol: 121.9mg | Sodium: 631mg

INGREDIENTS

- 1 cup uncooked long grain white rice
- 2 cups water
- 2 1/2 tablespoons garlic oil
- 2 (6 ounce) fillets salmon
- 1/4 teaspoon salt and pepper to taste
- 1/2 teaspoon dried dill weed
- 1/4 teaspoon paprika to taste

- 2 fresh tomatoes, diced
- 1 1/2 teaspoons minced garlic
- 1 teaspoon lemon juice
- 3 tablespoons chopped fresh parsley
- 1/4 cup grated Parmesan cheese
- 2 tablespoons butter
- 4 dashes hot pepper sauce

DIRECTIONS

1. In a medium saucepan, bring the rice and water to a boil. Reduce heat to low, cover, and cook 20 minutes.
2. Heat the garlic oil in a skillet over medium heat. Season the salmon with salt, pepper, dill, and paprika, and cook in the hot oil 1 to 2 minutes on each side, until tender enough to break apart. Break salmon into cubes with a spatula or fork. Mix in the tomatoes, garlic, and lemon juice. Continue cooking until salmon is easily flaked with a fork.
3. Mix the parsley, Parmesan cheese, butter, and hot pepper sauce into the skillet, and continue cooking 1 to 2 minutes, until well mixed. Serve over the cooked rice.

PEANUT BUTTER AND BANANA FRENCH TOAST

Servings: 2 | Prep: 10m | Cooks: 5m | Total: 15m

NUTRITION FACTS

Calories: 346.1 | Carbohydrates: 27.6g | Protein: 9.8g | Cholesterol: 123.5mg | Sodium: 362.2mg

INGREDIENTS

- 1 egg
- 1 dash vanilla extract
- 2 tablespoons creamy peanut butter
- 2 slices bread
- 1 small banana, sliced
- 2 tablespoons butter

DIRECTIONS

1. In a small bowl, lightly beat the egg and vanilla together.
2. Spread 1 tablespoon of peanut butter on top of each slice of bread. Place the banana slices on top of one of the slices of bread. Place the other slice of bread on top of the first, to make a peanut butter and banana sandwich.
3. In a skillet or frying pan, melt the butter over medium heat. Dip the sandwich into the egg mixture and place in the heated skillet. Cook until brown on both sides. Serve hot.

POTATO SKILLET

Servings: 6 | Prep: 10m | Cooks: 30m | Total: 40m

NUTRITION FACTS

Calories: 484.7 | Carbohydrates: 16g | Protein: 20.8g | Cholesterol: 331.9mg | Sodium: 836.6mg

INGREDIENTS

- 4 slices bacon

- 2 medium (2-1/4" to 3" dia, raw)s peeled and diced potatoes

- 1/8 teaspoon garlic salt

- 1/8 teaspoon seasoning salt

- 1/8 teaspoon black pepper

- 3 eggs, beaten

- 1/4 cup shredded Cheddar cheese

DIRECTIONS

1. Place bacon in a large, deep skillet. Cook over medium-high heat until evenly brown. Remove bacon slices, reserving grease. Crumble bacon and set aside.
2. Add potatoes to bacon grease and season with garlic salt, seasoned salt and black pepper. Cook until potatoes are soft.
3. When potatoes are tender, add crumbled bacon. Pour eggs over potatoes and cook until firm. Spread with cheese and cover with lid until melted.

PARMESAN-CRUSTED PORK CHOPS

Servings: 2 | Prep: 10m | Cooks: 35m | Total: 45m

NUTRITION FACTS

Calories: 245.9 | Carbohydrates: 1.2g | Protein: 30.5g | Cholesterol: 160.6mg | Sodium: 458.7mg

INGREDIENTS

- 1 serving cooking spray

- 1 egg

- 1/2 cup grated Parmesan cheese

- 1 teaspoon Cajun seasoning

- 2 eaches boneless pork chops, trimmed

DIRECTIONS

1. Preheat oven to 350 degrees F (175 degrees C). Spray a baking dish with cooking spray.
2. Whisk egg in a shallow bowl.
3. Mix Parmesan cheese and Cajun seasoning together on a plate.
4. Dip each pork chop into egg. Press into Parmesan mixture until coated on both sides. Place in the prepared baking dish.

5. Bake in the preheated oven until golden and an instant-read thermometer inserted into the center reads at least 145 degrees F (63 degrees C), 35 to 40 minutes.

CHICKEN, ASPARAGUS, AND MUSHROOM SKILLET

Servings: 2 | Prep: 15m | Cooks: 25m | Total: 40m

NUTRITION FACTS

Calories: 429.9 | Carbohydrates: 7.3g | Protein: 26.9g | Cholesterol: 106.6mg | Sodium: 491mg

INGREDIENTS

- 3 tablespoons butter
- 2 tablespoons olive oil
- 1/2 teaspoon dried parsley
- 1/2 teaspoon dried basil
- 1/8 teaspoon dried oregano
- 1 1/2 cloves garlic, minced
- 1/4 teaspoon salt
- 1 1/2 teaspoons lemon juice
- 1 1/2 teaspoons white cooking wine
- 2 skinless, boneless chicken breast halves, sliced
- 1/2 pound fresh asparagus, trimmed and cut into thirds
- 1 cup sliced fresh mushrooms

DIRECTIONS

1. Melt the butter with the olive oil in a skillet over medium-high; stir the parsley, basil, oregano, garlic, salt, lemon juice, and wine into the butter mixture. Add the chicken; cook and stir until the chicken is browned, about 3 minutes. Reduce heat to medium; cook, stirring occasionally, until the chicken is no longer pink inside, about 10 more minutes.
2. Add the asparagus; cook and stir until the asparagus is bright green and just starting to become tender, about 3 minutes. Stir in the mushrooms and cook an additional 3 minutes to let the mushrooms release their juice. Serve hot.

GNOCCHI WITH SAGE-BUTTER SAUCE

Servings: 2 | Prep: 10m | Cooks: 10m | Total: 20m

NUTRITION FACTS

Calories: 768.2 | Carbohydrates: 61.6g | Protein: 15.7g | Cholesterol: 140.2mg | Sodium: 977.4mg

INGREDIENTS

- 2 (12 ounce) packages potato gnocchi
- 1/4 cup butter
- 1 clove garlic, minced
- 1 teaspoon dried sage
- 1/4 teaspoon salt
- 1/4 cup grated Parmesan cheese
- 1/4 teaspoon ground black pepper
- 2 tablespoons grated Parmesan cheese

DIRECTIONS

1. Bring a large pot of lightly salted water to a boil over high heat. Add the gnocchi pasta, and cook until they float to the surface, 2 to 3 minutes; drain.
2. Melt the butter in a skillet over medium heat. Stir in the garlic, and cook until the garlic has softened and is beginning to turn golden brown, about 4 minutes. Stir in the sage and salt for a few seconds, then add the cooked gnocchi. Toss gently with 1/4 cup of Parmesan cheese and the pepper. Sprinkle with the remaining 2 tablespoons Parmesan cheese to serve.

BLUE CHEESE, BACON AND CHIVE STUFFED PORK CHOPS

Servings: 2 | Prep: 15m | Cooks: 20m | Total: 35m

NUTRITION FACTS

Calories: 361.8 | Carbohydrates: 2g | Protein: 33.8g | Cholesterol: 101.3mg | Sodium: 992.5mg

INGREDIENTS

- 2 raw chop with refuse, 195 g; yields excluding refuses boneless pork loin chops, butterflied
- 4 ounces crumbled blue cheese
- 2 slices bacon - cooked and crumbled
- 2 tablespoons chopped fresh chives
- 1 pinch garlic salt to taste
- 1 pinch ground black pepper to taste
- 1 tablespoon chopped fresh parsley for garnish

DIRECTIONS

1. Preheat the oven to 325 degrees F (165 degrees C). Grease a shallow baking dish.

2. In a small bowl, mix together the blue cheese, bacon and chives. Divide into halves, and pack each half into a loose ball. Place each one into a pocket of a butterflied pork chop, close, and secure with toothpicks. Season each chop with garlic salt and pepper. Keep in mind that the blue cheese will be salty. Place in the prepared baking dish.

3. Bake for 20 minutes in the preheated oven, or it may take longer if your chops are thicker. Cook until the stuffing is hot, and chops are to your desired degree of doneness. Garnish with fresh parsley and serve.

SIMPLE LEMON HERB CHICKEN

Servings: 2 | Prep: 10m | Cooks: 15m | Total: 25m

NUTRITION FACTS

Calories: 211.9 | Carbohydrates: 7.9g | Protein: 28.8g | Cholesterol: 68.4mg | Sodium: 94.2mg

INGREDIENTS

- 2 skinless, boneless chicken breast halves
- 1 lemon
- salt and pepper to taste
- 1 tablespoon olive oil
- 1 pinch dried oregano
- 2 sprigs fresh parsley, for garnish

DIRECTIONS

1. Cut lemon in half, and squeeze juice from 1/2 lemon on chicken. Season with salt to taste. Let sit while you heat oil in a small skillet over medium low heat.

2. When oil is hot, put chicken in skillet. As you saute chicken, add juice from other 1/2 lemon, pepper to taste, and oregano. Saute for 5 to 10 minutes each side, or until juices run clear. Serve with parsley for garnish.

DOMINICAN STYLE OATMEAL

Servings: 2 | Prep: 10m | Cooks: 5m | Total: 15m

NUTRITION FACTS

Calories: 220.1 | Carbohydrates: 35.3g | Protein: 8.7g | Cholesterol: 14.6mg | Sodium: 153.9mg

INGREDIENTS

- 1 1/2 cups milk
- 1/2 cup quick cooking
- 1 pinch ground nutmeg
- 1 pinch salt

oats

- 2 tablespoons white sugar
- 1/4 teaspoon ground cinnamon
- 1/4 teaspoon lemon zest

DIRECTIONS

1. Combine milk, oats, sugar, cinnamon, nutmeg, and salt in a saucepan. Add lemon peel, if using. Bring to a boil, stirring constantly for 2 minutes.

FAVORITE BARBECUE CHICKEN

Servings: 2 | Prep: 5m | Cooks: 35m | Total: 40m

NUTRITION FACTS

Calories: 4551.9 | Carbohydrates: 60.1g | Protein: 25.7g | Cholesterol: 67.2mg | Sodium: 714.1mg

INGREDIENTS

- 1 1/2 tablespoons olive oil
- 1/4 cup diced onion
- 2 cloves garlic, minced
- 5 tablespoons ketchup
- 3 tablespoons honey
- 3 tablespoons brown sugar
- 2 tablespoons apple cider vinegar
- 1 tablespoon Worcestershire sauce
- 1/8 teaspoon salt and pepper to taste
- 2 skinless, boneless chicken breast halves

DIRECTIONS

1. Preheat grill for medium-high heat.
2. Heat olive oil in a skillet over medium heat. Saute onion and garlic until tender. Stir in ketchup, honey, brown sugar, apple cider vinegar, Worcestershire sauce, salt, and pepper. Cook for a few minutes to thicken sauce. Remove from heat, and allow to cool.
3. Lightly oil the grill grate. Dip chicken in sauce, and turn to coat. Cook on grill for 10 to 15 minutes, turning once. Move chicken to the skillet with sauce. Simmer over medium heat for about 5 minutes on each side.

PORK FRIED RICE

Servings: 2 | Prep: 15m | Cooks: 15m | Total: 30m

NUTRITION FACTS

Calories: 556.6 | Carbohydrates: 80.7g | Protein: 26.1g | Cholesterol: 136.6mg

INGREDIENTS

- 1 tablespoon butter
- 1 (6 ounce) boneless pork loin chop, cut into small pieces
- 1/4 cup chopped carrot
- 1/4 cup chopped broccoli
- 1 green onion, chopped
- 1 egg, beaten
- 1 cup cold cooked rice
- 1/4 cup frozen peas
- 1 1/2 tablespoons soy sauce
- 1/8 teaspoon garlic powder
- 1/8 teaspoon ground ginger

DIRECTIONS

1. Melt butter in a large non-stick skillet over medium heat. Cook and stir pork, carrot, broccoli, peas, and green onion in melted butter until pork is cooked through, 7 to 10 minutes. Remove pork mixture to a bowl and return skillet to medium heat.
2. Scramble egg in the skillet until completely set. Return the pork mixture to the skillet. Stir rice, peas, soy sauce, garlic powder, and ground ginger into the pork mixture; cook and stir until heated through, 7 to 10 minutes.

CHICKEN BREASTS WITH CHIPOTLE GREEN ONION GRAVY

Servings: 2 | Prep: 5m | Cooks: 15m | Total: 20m

NUTRITION FACTS

Calories: 332.9 | Carbohydrates: 4.1g | Protein: 28.3g | Cholesterol: 103.9mg | Sodium: 187.7mg

INGREDIENTS

- 2 skinless, boneless chicken breast halves
- 1 tablespoon all-purpose flour

"

- 1 pinch salt and fresh ground pepper to taste
- 1 tablespoon olive oil
- 2 tablespoons butter
- 3/4 cup chicken broth
- 2 tablespoons minced green onions
- 1/2 teaspoon chipotle chile powder, or more to taste

DIRECTIONS

1. Place chicken breast halves between two sheets of heavy plastic (resealable freezer bags work well) on a solid, level surface. Firmly pound chicken with the smooth side of a meat mallet to a thickness of 1/2-inch. Season with salt and pepper to taste.
2. Heat olive oil in a skillet on high heat until it begins to shimmer, about 1 minute. Reduce heat to medium; cook chicken breasts until browned and no longer pink inside, about 5 minutes per side. Transfer cooked chicken to a warm plate and loosely cover with aluminum foil.
3. Melt butter in the skillet; stir in flour and cook for about 2 minutes. Stir in chicken broth, scraping up any browned bits from the bottom of the pan; cook and stir until gravy begins to simmer and thicken, 1 to 2 minutes.
4. Stir in green onions and chipotle chile powder.
5. Return chicken breasts to the skillet and cook until heated through, 1 to 2 minutes.

SIMPLE STROMBOLI

Servings: 3 | Prep: 10m | Cooks: 30m | Total: 40m

NUTRITION FACTS

Calories: 1064.8 | Carbohydrates: 77.8g | Protein: 59g | Cholesterol: 161.9mg | Sodium: 3633.1mg

INGREDIENTS

- 1/2 pound bulk pork sausage
- 1 (1 pound) loaf frozen bread dough, thawed
- 4 slices hard salami
- 4 slices thinly sliced ham
- 4 slices American cheese
- 1 cup shredded mozzarella cheese
- 1 pinch salt and ground black pepper to taste
- 1 egg white, lightly beaten

DIRECTIONS

1. Preheat oven to 425 degrees F (220 degrees C).

2. Heat a large skillet over medium-high heat; cook and stir sausage until crumbly, evenly browned, and no longer pink, about 10 minutes. Drain and discard any excess grease.
3. Pat out bread dough on an ungreased baking sheet, to 3/4-inch thickness. Lay salami, ham, and American cheese slices in center of dough. Sprinkle with mozzarella cheese, salt, pepper, and cooked sausage. Wrap dough to cover ingredients, pinching and sealing edges to prevent leakage; brush top with egg white.
4. Bake in preheated oven until dough is baked and lightly browned, 17 to 20 minutes.

SALMON

Servings: 2 | Prep: 10m | Cooks: 15m | Total: 25m

NUTRITION FACTS

Calories: 496 | Carbohydrates: 2.6g | Fat: 33g | Protein: 45.1g | Cholesterol: 132mg | Sodium: 520mg

INGREDIENTS

- 2 (8 ounce) center-cut salmon fillets, with skin
- 1/4 teaspoon kosher salt
- 1 teaspoon vegetable oil
- 1 clove garlic, sliced
- 1 tablespoon chopped fresh tarragon
- 1 tablespoon chopped fresh flat-leaf parsley
- 3 tablespoons mayonnaise
- 1 teaspoon Dijon mustard
- 1 teaspoon fresh lemon juice
- 1 pinch cayenne pepper

DIRECTIONS

1. Season salmon fillets with kosher salt. Line a baking baking sheet with foil and brush lightly with vegetable oil.
2. Preheat oven's broiler on high and set the oven rack about 8 inches from the heat source.
3. Process garlic, tarragon, and parsley in a blender or mortar and pestle to form a loose paste.
4. Mix mayonnaise, Dijon mustard, lemon juice, and cayenne pepper into garlic paste until combined.
5. Place salmon fillets skin side down on the baking sheet. Spoon herb spread over the top and sides of each fillet.
6. Cook under the preheated broiler until fillets are well-browned, about 5 minutes. Turn the broiler off and turn the oven to 350 degrees F (175 degrees C).
7. Bake until the internal temperature of the salmon is 130 degrees F (55 degrees C) and salmon flakes easily with a fork, about 3 to 4 minutes.

TOMATO BASIL SALMON

Servings: 2 | Prep: 10m | Cooks: 20m | Total: 30m

NUTRITION FACTS

Calories: 405 | Carbohydrates: 4g | Fat: 26.6g | Protein: 36.2g | Cholesterol: 104mg

INGREDIENTS

- 2 (6 ounce) boneless salmon fillets
- 1 tablespoon dried basil
- 1 tomato, thinly sliced
- 1 tablespoon olive oil
- 2 tablespoons grated Parmesan cheese

DIRECTIONS

1. Preheat oven to 375 degrees F (190 degrees C). Line a baking sheet with a piece of aluminum foil, and spray with nonstick cooking spray. Place the salmon fillets onto the foil, sprinkle with basil, top with tomato slices, drizzle with olive oil, and sprinkle with the Parmesan cheese.
2. Bake in the preheated oven until the salmon is opaque in the center, and the Parmesan cheese is lightly browned on top, about 20 minutes.

SAUSAGE-STUFFED EGGPLANT

Servings: 2 | Prep: 15m | Cooks: 1h | Total: 1h15m

NUTRITION FACTS

Calories: 835.9 | Carbohydrates: 64.2g | Protein: 40.7g | Cholesterol: 178.8mg | Sodium: 2410.9mg

INGREDIENTS

- 1 (1 1/2 pound) eggplant, halved lengthwise
- 1 tablespoon olive oil
- 1/2 pound bulk Italian sausage
- 1/4 teaspoon garlic powder
- 1/4 teaspoon dried Italian seasoning
- 1/8 teaspoon black pepper
- 2 tablespoons dry bread crumbs
- 2 cups spaghetti sauce, divided
- 1 cup mozzarella cheese, divided
- 1 egg, beaten

DIRECTIONS

1. Preheat oven to 400 degrees F (200 degrees C).
2. Brush cut sides of eggplant with olive oil and place, cut-side up onto a baking sheet. Roast in preheated oven for 30 minutes, then remove and allow to cool slightly.
3. Meanwhile, brown the Italian sausage in a skillet over medium-high heat; drain off the grease. Place into a mixing bowl, and season with garlic powder, Italian seasoning, and pepper. Stir in bread crumbs, 1/2 cup of spaghetti sauce, 1/2 cup of mozzarella cheese, and the beaten egg; mix well.
4. Once the roasted eggplant has cooled enough to handle, scoop out the flesh to within 1/2-inch of the skin to create a shell. Roughly chop the eggplant meat, and fold into the sausage mixture. Divide evenly among the two eggplant shells, and sprinkle with remaining mozzarella cheese.
5. Bake in preheated oven until the filling has set, and the cheese is bubbly and golden-brown, about 30 minutes. While the eggplant is baking, warm the remaining spaghetti sauce in a saucepan over medium-low heat to serve with the eggplant.

SPOILED BABY BACK RIBS

Servings: 3 | Prep: 10m | Cooks: 1h15m | Total: 1h25m

NUTRITION FACTS

Calories: 893.8 | Carbohydrates: 36.9g | Protein: 49.5g | Cholesterol: 234mg | Sodium: 1650.5mg

INGREDIENTS

- 3 pounds pork back ribs, cut into serving size pieces
- 1 cup ketchup
- 1/4 cup apple cider vinegar
- 3 tablespoons Worcestershire sauce
- 3 tablespoons brown sugar
- 1/2 teaspoon salt
- 1 teaspoon liquid smoke flavoring

DIRECTIONS

1. Place the ribs into a large pot and cover with water. Bring to a boil over high heat; reduce heat to medium and simmer until tender, about 1 hour. Meanwhile, stir the ketchup, vinegar, Worcestershire sauce, sugar, salt, and liquid smoke in a saucepan. Bring to a simmer over medium-high heat; reduce heat to medium-low and simmer uncovered, stirring frequently, until thickened, about 30 minutes.
2. Preheat the oven's broiler and set the oven rack about 6 inches from the heat source. Line a baking sheet with foil.
3. Drain the ribs and place meaty-side-up onto the prepared baking sheet. Brush the ribs with half of the barbeque sauce. Broil in the preheated oven until the sauce has turned sticky and lightly

browned, about 7 minutes. Turn the ribs over and brush with the remaining sauce. Continue to broil until the sauce has turned sticky, about 7 minutes.

FIRE ROASTED TOMATO AND FETA PASTA WITH SHRIMP

Servings: 2 | Prep: 15m | Cooks: 12m | Total: 27m

NUTRITION FACTS

Calories: 702 | Carbohydrates: 94.8g | Fat: 23.4g | Protein: 31.8g | Cholesterol: 111mg

| Sodium: 1354mg

INGREDIENTS

- 1/2 pound linguine pasta
- 1 tablespoon olive oil
- 3 cloves garlic, minced
- 12 medium shrimp, peeled and deveined
- 1 (14.5 ounce) can fire roasted tomatoes
- 1 tablespoon chopped fresh basil
- salt and pepper to taste
- 1/2 cup crumbled feta cheese

DIRECTIONS

1. Bring a large pot of lightly salted water to a boil. Add pasta and cook for 8 to 10 minutes or until al dente; drain.
2. While the pasta is cooking, heat the olive oil in a large skillet over medium heat. Add the garlic; cook and stir until fragrant, about 1 minute. Add the shrimp, and cook until opaque, about 3 to 5 minutes. Pour in the tomatoes and heat through. Season with basil, salt and pepper.
3. Toss the cooked pasta in the sauce, and sprinkle with crumbled feta to serve.

MEN LOVE THIS STEAK

Servings: 2 | Prep: 10m | Cooks: 14m | Total: 24m

NUTRITION FACTS

Calories: 667.7 | Carbohydrates: 7.5g | Protein: 37.3g | Cholesterol: 137mg | Sodium: 1204.4mg

INGREDIENTS

- 2 (8 ounce) beef rib-eye steaks, cut 3/4 inch thick
- 3/4 teaspoon Dijon mustard

- 1 teaspoon steak seasoning
- 3 thick slices bacon
- 2 teaspoons butter
- 1/4 teaspoon Worcestershire sauce
- 1/2 cup thinly sliced red bell pepper
- 8 ounces small mushrooms, quartered
- 2 tablespoons crumbled blue cheese

DIRECTIONS

1. Prepare an outdoor grill using charcoal briquettes stacked 2 to 3 deep. Season the steaks on both sides with steak seasoning.
2. While the charcoal heats up, fry the bacon in a skillet over medium-high heat until crisp. Remove from the skillet and drain on paper towels. Leave grease in the pan.
3. When the charcoal is covered with gray ashes, put the steaks on the grill. Cook for 12 minutes, turning once, or to your desired degree of doneness.
4. While the steaks are cooking, stir the butter, Worcestershire sauce and mustard into the bacon grease. Cook and stir over medium-high heat until butter has melted. Add the red bell pepper and mushrooms; cook and stir until tender.
5. To serve, place steaks onto plates. Top with bacon, then blue cheese and then the vegetables. Serve immediately.

FETA AND BACON STUFFED CHICKEN WITH ONION MASHED POTATOES

Servings: 3 | Prep: 30m | Cooks: 35m | Total: 1h5m

NUTRITION FACTS

Calories: 1497.9 | Carbohydrates: 118.9g | Protein: 64.7g | Cholesterol: 343.3mg | Sodium: 1960.6mg

INGREDIENTS

- 3/4 pound bacon, cut into 1 inch pieces
- 1 cup crumbled feta cheese
- 3 tablespoons sour cream
- 1/8 tablespoon dried oregano
- 1/8 teaspoon ground black pepper
- 2 eggs, beaten
- 1 cup dry bread crumbs
- 4 medium (2-1/4" to 3" dia, raw)s potatoes, peeled and cubed
- 1 sweet onion (such as Vidalia), chopped
- 2 tablespoons butter

- 3 (4 ounce) skinless, boneless chicken breast halves
- 1 cup all-purpose flour
- 3 tablespoons sour cream

DIRECTIONS

1. Preheat an oven to 350 degrees F (175 degrees C). Place the bacon in a large, deep skillet, and cook over medium-high heat, turning occasionally, until evenly browned but still soft. Reserve the bacon grease in the skillet, and cool the bacon slices on a paper towel-lined plate. Once cool, mix the bacon together with the feta cheese, 3 tablespoons of sour cream, oregano, and black pepper in a small bowl; set aside.
2. Lay a chicken breast flat onto your work surface. Use the tip of a sharp boning or paring knife to cut a 2-inch pocket in the chicken breast. Repeat with the remaining chicken breasts. Spoon the bacon mixture into the pockets. Pour the flour, egg, and bread crumbs into separate, shallow dishes. Gently press the chicken breasts into the flour to coat. Dip each into the beaten egg, then press into bread crumbs.
3. Reheat the bacon grease over medium heat. Brown the chicken breasts on both sides in the hot fat, about 2 minutes per side. Reserve the bacon grease in the pan. Place the breasts on a baking dish, and bake in the preheated oven until the chicken is no longer pink and the filling is hot, 20 to 25 minutes. An instant-read thermometer inserted into the center should read at least 165 degrees F (74 degrees C).
4. Meanwhile, place the potatoes into a large pot and cover with salted water. Bring to a boil over high heat, then reduce heat to medium-low, cover, and simmer until tender, about 20 minutes. Drain.
5. While the potatoes are boiling, cook the onion in the remaining bacon grease over medium heat until very tender and golden brown, about 10 minutes. Once the potatoes are done, mash together with the onion, butter, and remaining 3 tablespoons of sour cream. Serve the chicken breasts accompanied by the mashed potatoes.

ONION PAN-FRIED PORK CHOPS

Servings: 2 | Prep: 5m | Cooks: 10m | Total: 15m

NUTRITION FACTS

Calories: 317.4 | Carbohydrates: 20.7g | Protein: 16.8g | Cholesterol: 38.2mg | Sodium: 1264.2mg

INGREDIENTS

- 1 (1 ounce) envelope dry onion soup mix
- 1/4 cup all-purpose flour
- 2 pork chops
- 1 cup olive oil for frying

DIRECTIONS

1. Before opening the onion soup mix, use your hands to crush the larger bits of onion in the packet. Open the packet, and pour the mix into a shallow bowl. Stir in the flour.
2. Heat the oil in a heavy skillet over medium heat. The oil is hot enough when a pinch of the flour mixture sizzles when tossed into the oil. Coat pork chops in the onion soup mixture, and shake off the excess. Carefully place in the hot oil. Turn chops over after about 30 seconds to quickly sear both sides. Cook for about 4 minutes per side, or to desired degree of doneness.

CREAMY CHEESY SCRAMBLED EGGS WITH BASIL

Servings: 2 | Prep: 5m | Cooks: 10m | Total: 15m

NUTRITION FACTS

Calories: 297.1 | Carbohydrates: 2.5g | Protein: 20.2g | Cholesterol: 410.3mg | Sodium: 432.7mg

INGREDIENTS

- 4 eggs
- 3 tablespoons sour cream
- 1/2 cup shredded mozzarella cheese
- 1 pinch salt and pepper to taste
- 2 teaspoons butter
- 1 tablespoon minced fresh basil

DIRECTIONS

1. Whisk eggs and sour cream in a bowl until creamy and smooth. Mix in cheese. Season with salt and pepper.
2. Melt butter in a skillet over medium heat. Pour in egg mixture; cook, stirring constantly, until eggs reach the desired consistency. Mix in basil during final minutes of cooking.

PAN SEARED RED SNAPPER

Servings: 2 | Prep: 10m | Cooks: 10m | Total: 20m

NUTRITION FACTS

Calories: 224.3 | Carbohydrates: 16.5g | Protein: 24g | Cholesterol: 41.4mg | Sodium: 138.7mg

INGREDIENTS

- 2 (4 ounce) fillets red snapper
- 1 tablespoon olive oil
- 1 teaspoon Dijon mustard
- 1 tablespoon honey

- 1 lemon, juiced
- 2 tablespoons rice wine vinegar
- 1/4 cup chopped green onions
- 1 teaspoon ground ginger

DIRECTIONS

1. Rinse snapper under cold water, and pat dry. In a shallow bowl, mix together olive oil, lemon juice, rice vinegar, mustard, honey, green onions, and ginger.
2. Heat a non-stick skillet over medium heat. Dip snapper fillets in marinade to coat both sides, and place in skillet. Cook for 2 to 3 minutes on each side. Pour remaining marinade into skillet. Reduce heat, and simmer for 2 to 3 minutes, or until fish flakes easily with a fork.

SLOW COOKER SPICY CHICKEN

Servings: 3 | Prep: 15m | Cooks: 4h | Total: 4h15m

NUTRITION FACTS

Calories: 152 | Carbohydrates: 7.1g | Protein: 24.4g | Cholesterol: 60.8mg | Sodium: 392.1mg

INGREDIENTS

- 3 skinless, boneless chicken breast halves
- 1/2 (8 ounce) jar medium salsa
- 1/4 cup tomato sauce
- 2 cloves garlic, minced
- 1 small red onion, chopped
- 1 teaspoon ground cumin
- 1 teaspoon chili powder
- 1 pinch salt and fresh ground pepper to tast

DIRECTIONS

1. Arrange the chicken breasts in the bottom of a slow cooker, and pour in the salsa and tomato sauce. Add the garlic and onion, and sprinkle in the cumin, chili powder, salt, and pepper. Set the cooker on Low, and cook until the chicken is very tender, 4 to 5 hours. Shred the chicken with two forks for serving.

EASY YET ROMANTIC FILET MIGNON

Servings: 2 | Prep: 5m | Cooks: 15m | Total: 20m

NUTRITION FACTS

Calories: 611 | Carbohydrates: 2.1g | Fat: 35g | Protein: 67.4g | Cholesterol: 196mg | Sodium: 444mg

INGREDIENTS

- 2 (8 ounce) (1 inch thick) filet mignon steaks
- 2 teaspoons olive oil
- 1/4 teaspoon onion powder
- Salt and pepper to taste
- 2 tablespoons minced shallot
- 2 slices bacon

DIRECTIONS

1. Place oven rack in its highest position. Set oven to Broil.
2. Rub steaks all over with olive oil. Sprinkle with onion powder, then with salt and pepper. Wrap one slice of bacon around each steak, and secure with a toothpick.
3. Place steaks onto a broiler pan, and broil for 5 to 7 minutes. Turn the steaks over, and sprinkle the tops with shallots. Broil for an additional 5 to 7 minutes, or until the steaks are cooked to your liking.

VERACRUZ-STYLE RED SNAPPER

Servings: 2 | Prep: 15m | Cooks: 25m | Total: 40m

NUTRITION FACTS

Calories: 452 | Carbohydrates: 16.2g | Fat: 25.2g | Protein: 43.1g | Cholesterol: 73mg | Sodium: 1034mg

INGREDIENTS

- 2 tablespoons olive oil
- 1/2 white onion, diced
- 3 cloves garlic, minced
- 1 tablespoon capers
- 1 tablespoon caper juice
- 1 cup cherry tomatoes, halved
- 1 jalapeno pepper, seeded and chopped
- 2 teaspoons chopped fresh oregano
- 2 teaspoons olive oil
- 2 (7 ounce) red snapper fillets, cut in half
- salt and pepper to taste
- 1/2 teaspoon cayenne pepper, or more to taste

- 1/3 cup pitted, sliced green olives (such as Castelvetrano)
- 2 limes, juiced

DIRECTIONS

1. Preheat oven to 425 degrees F (220 degrees C).
2. Heat olive oil in a skillet over medium heat. Stir in onion; cook and stir until onions begin to turn translucent, 6 to 7 minutes.
3. Cook and stir in garlic until fragrant, about 30 seconds. Add capers and caper juice; stir to combine.
4. Stir in tomatoes, olives, jalapeno pepper, . Cook and stir until jalapeno pepper softens and tomatoes begin to collapse, about 3 minutes. Remove from heat; stir in oregano.
5. Drizzle 1 teaspoon olive oil into a small baking dish. Sprinkle in 1 tablespoon of the tomato-olive mixture. Top with 1 snapper fillet, salt, black pepper, and cayenne pepper. Top with more filling and juice from 1 lime. Repeat with remaining snapper fillet, seasoning, and lime juice in a second baking dish.
6. Bake in the preheated oven until fish is flaky and no longer translucent, 15 to 20 minutes.

MAPLE CAJUN MAHI MAHI

Servings: 2 | Prep: 5m | Cooks: 10m | Total: 15m

NUTRITION FACTS

Calories: 218.7 | Carbohydrates: 15.6g | Protein: 21.1g | Cholesterol: 81.8mg | Sodium: 811.4mg

INGREDIENTS

- 1 tablespoon olive oil
- 2 tablespoons maple syrup
- 1 tablespoon Cajun seasoning
- 1/2 teaspoon garlic powder
- 2 (4 ounce) fillets mahi mahi fillets, rinsed and patted dry

DIRECTIONS

1. Heat the olive oil in a pan over medium-high heat.
2. Stir the maple syrup, Cajun seasoning, and garlic powder together in a small bowl.
3. Brush the maple syrup mixture over the mahi mahi fillets.
4. Cook the mahi mahi in the hot oil until the fish flakes easily with a fork, 3 to 5 minutes per side.

SPAGHETTI ALLA CARBONARA

Servings: 2 | Prep: 5m | Cooks: 20m | Total: 25m

NUTRITION FACTS

Calories: 688 | Carbohydrates: 66.1g | Fat: 30.3g | Protein: 36.3g | Cholesterol: 220mg | Sodium: 984mg

INGREDIENTS

- 4 ounces guanciale, cut into 1/4-inch cubes
- 1 tablespoon olive oil
- 1 teaspoon ground black pepper, or to taste
- 2 eggs
- 3 tablespoons grated Parmigiano-Reggiano cheese
- 3 tablespoons grated Pecorino Romano cheese
- 1 teaspoon ground black pepper, or to taste
- 6 ounces spaghetti
- 1 cup reserved pasta water
- 3 tablespoons grated Parmigiano-Reggiano cheese
- 3 tablespoons grated Pecorino Romano cheese

DIRECTIONS

1. Cook guanciale with olive oil and 1 teaspoon ground black pepper in a Dutch oven over medium-low heat until almost crisp, about 5 minutes. Reduce heat to low.
2. Whisk eggs, 3 tablespoons Parmigiano-Reggiano cheese, 3 tablespoons Pecorino Romano cheese, and 1 teaspoon ground black pepper in a bowl. Set aside.
3. Bring a large pot of lightly salted water to a boil. Cook spaghetti in the boiling water, stirring occasionally until cooked through but firm to the bite, 10 to 12 minutes. Drain, reserving 1 cup of the pasta water.
4. Pour reserved pasta water and drained spaghetti into the bacon-pepper mixture; stir to combine.
5. Slowly pour egg mixture into the pasta mixture; cook, stirring constantly until the egg mixture forms a thick sauce, 1 to 2 minutes. Remove from heat.
6. Stir remaining 3 tablespoons Parmigiano-Reggiano cheese and 3 tablespoons Pecorino Romano cheese into the pasta mixture and serve.

EGGPLANT SANDWICHES

Servings: 2 | Prep: 20m | Cooks: 10m | Total: 30m

NUTRITION FACTS

Calories: 802 | Carbohydrates: 91.3g | Protein: 23.8g | Cholesterol: 43.8mg | Sodium: 1460.2mg

INGREDIENTS

- 1 small eggplant, halved and sliced
- 1 tablespoon olive oil, or as needed
- 1/4 cup mayonnaise
- 2 cloves garlic, minced
- 2 (6 inch) French sandwich rolls
- 1 small tomato, sliced
- 1/2 cup crumbled feta cheese
- 1/4 cup chopped fresh basil leaves

DIRECTIONS

1. Preheat your oven's broiler. Brush eggplant slices with olive oil, and place them on a baking sheet or broiling pan. Place the pan about 6 inches from the heat source. Cook under the broiler for 10 minutes, or until tender and toasted.
2. Split the French rolls lengthwise, and toast. In a cup or small bowl, stir together the mayonnaise and garlic. Spread this mixture on the toasted bread. Fill the rolls with eggplant slices, tomato, feta cheese and basil leaves.

BAKED FALAFEL

Servings: 2 | Prep: 20m | Cooks: 20m | Total: 55m | Additional: 15m

NUTRITION FACTS

Calories: 281.1 | Carbohydrates: 39.3g | Protein: 11.4g | Cholesterol: 93mg | Sodium: 909.4mg

INGREDIENTS

- 1/4 cup chopped onion
- 1 (15 ounce) can garbanzo beans, rinsed and drained
- 1/4 cup chopped fresh parsley
- 3 cloves garlic, minced
- 1 teaspoon ground cumin
- 1/4 teaspoon ground coriander
- 1/4 teaspoon salt
- 1/4 teaspoon baking soda
- 1 tablespoon all-purpose flour
- 1 egg, beaten
- 2 teaspoons olive oil

DIRECTIONS

1. Wrap onion in cheese cloth and squeeze out as much moisture as possible. Set aside. Place garbanzo beans, parsley, garlic, cumin, coriander, salt, and baking soda in a food processor. Process until the mixture is coarsely pureed. Mix garbanzo bean mixture and onion together in a bowl. Stir in the flour and egg. Shape mixture into four large patties and let stand for 15 minutes.
2. Preheat an oven to 400 degrees F (200 degrees C).
3. Heat olive oil in a large, oven-safe skillet over medium-high heat. Place the patties in the skillet; cook until golden brown, about 3 minutes on each side.
4. Transfer skillet to the preheated oven and bake until heated through, about 10 minutes.

MUSTARD CRUSTED TILAPIA

Servings: 2 | Prep: 5m | Cooks: 15m | Total: 20m

NUTRITION FACTS

Calories: 181.1 | Carbohydrates: 2g | Protein: 35.1g | Cholesterol: 62.1mg | Sodium: 151.2mg

INGREDIENTS

- 2 (6 ounce) fresh tilapia fillets
- 1 teaspoon spicy brown mustard
- 1 teaspoon Worcestershire sauce
- 1/2 teaspoon lemon juice
- 1/4 teaspoon garlic powder
- 1/4 teaspoon dried oregano
- 1/2 teaspoon grated Parmesan cheese
- 1 teaspoon fine Italian bread crumbs

DIRECTIONS

1. Preheat oven to 375 degrees F (190 degrees C). Spray a glass baking dish with cooking spray.
2. Place tilapia fillets into prepared baking dish, and bake in preheated oven for 10 minutes. Meanwhile, stir together the mustard, Worcestershire sauce, lemon juice, garlic powder, oregano, and Parmesan cheese.
3. When fish has cooked for 10 minutes, spread with herb paste, and sprinkle with bread crumbs. Continue baking for another 5 minutes until the topping is bubbly and golden.

GARLIC CHICKEN FRIED BROWN RICE

Servings: 3 | Prep: 20m | Cooks: 15m | Total: 35m

NUTRITION FACTS

Calories: 444.4 | Carbohydrates: 57.4g | Protein: 24.3g | Cholesterol: 43.1mg | Sodium: 701.4mg

INGREDIENTS

- 2 tablespoons vegetable oil, divided
- 8 ounces skinless, boneless chicken breast, cut into strips
- 1/2 red bell pepper, chopped
- 1/2 cup green onion, chopped
- 4 cloves garlic, minced
- 3 cups cooked brown rice
- 2 tablespoons light soy sauce
- 1 tablespoon rice vinegar
- 1 cup frozen peas, thawed

DIRECTIONS

1. Heat 1 tablespoon of vegetable oil in a large skillet set over medium heat. Add the chicken, bell pepper, green onion and garlic. Cook and stir until the chicken is cooked through, about 5 minutes. Remove the chicken to a plate and keep warm.
2. Heat the remaining tablespoon of oil in the same skillet over medium-high heat. Add the rice; cook and stir to heat through. Stir in the soy sauce, rice vinegar and peas, and continue to cook for 1 minute. Return the chicken mixture to the skillet and stir to blend with the rice and heat through before serving.

LUCKY'S QUICKIE CHICKIE

Servings: 2 | Prep: 10m | Cooks: 10m | Total: 20m

NUTRITION FACTS

Calories: 156.5 | Carbohydrates: 5.3g | Protein: 17.8g | Cholesterol: 48.5mg | Sodium: 334.3mg

INGREDIENTS

- 2 teaspoons olive oil
- 6 ounces chicken tenderloin strips
- 1/4 teaspoon salt
- 1/8 teaspoon freshly ground black pepper
- 2 tablespoons chopped fresh basil
- 1 1/2 teaspoons honey
- 1 1/2 teaspoons balsamic vinegar, or more to taste

DIRECTIONS

1. Heat olive oil in a nonstick skillet over medium-high heat. Season chicken with salt and pepper. Cook and stir chicken in the hot oil until chicken is no longer pink in the center, about 3 to 5 minutes. Stir basil, honey, and balsamic vinegar into chicken and cook for 1 more minute.

GORGONZOLA STUFFED CHICKEN BREASTS WRAPPED IN BACON

Servings: 2 | Prep: 20m | Cooks: 35m | Total: 55m

NUTRITION FACTS

Calories: 336.7 | Carbohydrates: 2.8g | Protein: 37.8g | Cholesterol: 112.7mg | Sodium: 885.8mg

INGREDIENTS

- 2 skinless, boneless chicken breast halves
- 1/4 cup crumbled Gorgonzola cheese
- 2 tablespoons minced fresh parsley
- 2 tablespoons minced shallot
- 1 clove garlic, minced
- 4 thick bacon slices thick slices of applewood smoked bacon
- 1 pinch salt and ground black pepper to taste

DIRECTIONS

1. Preheat oven to 375 degrees F (190 degrees C). Spray an 8x8-inch baking dish with cooking spray.
2. Using a sharp knife, cut a slit into the thick side of each chicken breast about 2 inches long and 1 1/2 inches deep.
3. Mash together the Gorgonzola cheese, parsley, shallot, and garlic in a small bowl; season with salt and black pepper. Divide the filling in half, and stuff each chicken breast with cheese filling. Wrap 2 slices of bacon around each breast, and secure with wooden toothpicks. Place the chicken breasts into the prepared baking dish.
4. Bake in the preheated oven until the bacon is browned and the chicken is no longer pink inside, about 35 minutes. An instant-read thermometer inserted into the center of a breast should read about 165 degrees F (75 degrees C).

DRUNKEN MUSSELS

Servings: 2 | Prep: 10m | Cooks: 10m | Total: 20m

NUTRITION FACTS

Calories: 553 | Carbohydrates: 40.5g | Fat: 14.8g | Protein: 28.1g | Cholesterol: mg

INGREDIENTS

- 2 tablespoons butter
- 4 cloves garlic, minced
- 1/2 teaspoon red pepper flakes, or to taste
- 1 lemon, zested
- 2 cups white wine
- freshly ground black pepper to taste
- 2 pounds mussels, cleaned and debearded
- 1 cup chopped fresh flat-leaf parsley
- 2 slices bread, grilled
- 2 lemon wedges for garnish

DIRECTIONS

1. Melt butter in a large stock pot over medium heat. Add garlic and let sizzle for about 30 seconds. Season with red pepper flakes and lemon zest, stirring for about 45 seconds.
2. Quickly pour in wine into the pan and season with black pepper. Bring sauce to a boil, stir in mussels, and cover immediately. Shake pot and let boil for 1 minute.
3. Stir mussels, replace cover, and let boil for 2 more minutes. The shells will begin to open. Stir in parsley, cover pot, and cook until all shells are open, 1 to 3 minutes.
4. Serve with grilled bread and lemon wedge.

QUICK LEMON DIJON CHICKEN

Servings: 2 | Prep: 10m | Cooks: 15m | Total: 25m

NUTRITION FACTS

Calories: 301.1 | Carbohydrates: 10.5g | Protein: 55g | Cholesterol: 136.9mg | Sodium: 983.6mg

INGREDIENTS

- 2 skinless, boneless chicken breast halves - cut into 2 inch pieces
- 1/4 lime, juiced
- 4 tablespoons Dijon mustard
- 1 pinch freshly ground black pepper

- 1/2 lemon, juiced
- 1 pinch Creole-style seasoning to taste

DIRECTIONS

1. Place chicken in a skillet over medium heat. Pour in lime and lemon juices, and stir in Dijon, black pepper, and Creole-seasoning. Cook, turning chicken occasionally, until the chicken pieces are done, about 15 minutes.

SEXY SHRIMP SCAMPI

Servings: 2 | Prep: 20m | Cooks: 15m | Total: 45m | Additional: 10m

NUTRITION FACTS

Calories: 342 | Carbohydrates: 1.2g | Fat: 26.3g | Protein: 24.8g | Cholesterol: 259mg | | Sodium: 825mg

INGREDIENTS

- 30 medium shrimp - peeled and deveined
- 2 tablespoons olive oil
- 2 tablespoons butter, melted
- 2 cloves garlic, minced
- 1/2 teaspoon kosher salt
- 1/2 teaspoon ground black pepper

DIRECTIONS

1. Preheat an oven to 350 degrees F (175 degrees C).
2. Toss the shrimp in a bowl with the olive oil, melted butter, garlic, salt, and pepper; set aside for 10 minutes. Arrange the shrimp in a circular pattern in a round casserole dish.
3. Bake in the preheated oven until the shrimp are pink and cooked through, about 15 minutes.

PAN SEARED LEMON TILAPIA WITH PARMESAN PASTA

Servings: 2 | Prep: 10m | Cooks: 10m | Total: 25m

NUTRITION FACTS

Calories: 554.9 | Carbohydrates: 44.8g | Protein: 34.8g | Cholesterol: 50.2mg | Sodium: 230.8mg

INGREDIENTS

- 4 ounces elbow macaroni
- 1 tablespoon light olive oil

- 2 tablespoons light olive oil
- 2 eaches tilapia fillets
- 1 tablespoon lemon juice
- 1/8 teaspoon dried oregano
- 1 pinch dried basil
- 1 pinch dried cilantro
- 1 pinch salt and ground black pepper
- ¼ cup freshly grated Parmesan cheese
- 1 teaspoon lemon juice
- 1 pinch garlic powder
- 1 pinch dried basil
- 1 pinch dried oregano
- 1 pinch dried cilantro
- 1 pinch salt and ground black pepper

DIRECTIONS

1. Bring a saucepan of lightly salted water to a boil over medium heat, stir in the macaroni, and return to a boil. Cook the macaroni uncovered, stirring occasionally, until it is cooked through but still firm to the bite, about 8 minutes. Drain well.
2. Meanwhile, heat 2 tablespoons of olive oil in a skillet over medium heat. Sprinkle both sides of the tilapia fillets with lemon juice, oregano, basil, cilantro, salt, and pepper, and lay the fillets in the heated skillet, making sure they don't touch. Sear the fillets for 2 to 4 minutes on each side, until the fish is golden brown on the outside, and opaque and flaky inside.
3. Return the hot, cooked macaroni to the saucepan, and stir in 1 tablespoon of olive oil to coat the pasta. Sprinkle on the Parmesan cheese, stir to mix, and stir in 1 teaspoon of lemon juice, the garlic powder, basil, oregano, cilantro, salt, and pepper. Divide the pasta between two plates, and top each with a tilapia fillet.

CRAB LEGS WITH GARLIC BUTTER SAUCE

Servings: 2 | Prep: 5m | Cooks: 15m | Total: 20m

NUTRITION FACTS

Calories: 520.1 | Carbohydrates: 1g | Protein: 43.6g | Cholesterol: 274.2mg | Sodium: 1030.7mg

INGREDIENTS

- 1 pound Snow Crab clusters, thawed if necessary
- 1/4 cup butter
- 1 clove garlic, minced
- 1 1/2 teaspoons dried parsley
- 1/8 teaspoon salt
- 1/4 teaspoon fresh-ground black pepper

DIRECTIONS

1. Cut a slit, length-wise, into the shell of each piece of crab.
2. Melt the butter in a large skillet over medium heat; cook the garlic in the butter until translucent; stir in the parsley, salt, and pepper. Continue to heat mixture until bubbling. Add the crab legs; toss to coat; allow to simmer in the butter mixture until completely heated, 5 to 6 minutes.

CORIANDER AND CUMIN RUBBED PORK CHOPS

Servings: 2 | Prep: 10m | Cooks: 15m | Total: 25m

NUTRITION FACTS

Calories: 278 | Carbohydrates: 4.8g | Fat: 22g | Protein: 15.5g | Cholesterol: 38mg | Sodium: 615mg

INGREDIENTS

- 1/2 teaspoon salt
- 1 tablespoon ground cumin
- 1 tablespoon ground coriander
- 3 cloves garlic, minced
- 2 tablespoons olive oil, divided
- 2 boneless pork loin chops
- ground black pepper to taste

DIRECTIONS

1. Mix the salt, cumin, coriander, garlic, and 1 tablespoon olive oil to form a paste. Season the pork chops with salt and pepper, and rub with the paste.
2. Heat the remaining olive oil in a skillet over medium heat, and cook the pork chops about 5 minutes on each side, to an internal temperature of 145 degrees F (63 degrees C).

PIZZA CHICKEN

Servings: 2 | Prep: 15m | Cooks: 30m | Total: 45m

NUTRITION FACTS

Calories: 551.7 | Carbohydrates: 52.9g | Protein: 46.2g | Cholesterol: 185.2mg | Sodium: 2497.3mg

INGREDIENTS

- 1/2 cup Italian-seasoned bread crumbs
- 1/4 cup grated Parmesan
- 1 tablespoon lemon juice
- 2 skinless, boneless

cheese

- 1 teaspoon salt

- 1 teaspoon ground black pepper

- 1/2 cup all-purpose flour

- 1 egg

chicken breast halves

- 1/2 cup pizza sauce, divided

- 1/2 cup shredded mozzarella cheese, divided

- 4 slices pepperoni, or to taste - divided

DIRECTIONS

1. Preheat oven to 400 degrees F (200 degrees C).
2. Combine bread crumbs, Parmesan cheese, salt, and black pepper in a shallow bowl; place flour into a second bowl. Whisk egg and lemon juice together in a third bowl.
3. Dip each chicken breast in egg mixture and dredge in flour; dip again in egg mixture and dredge chicken in crumb mixture until coated. Place coated chicken breasts into a baking dish.
4. Bake in the preheated oven until chicken is heated through and crumbs are golden, about 20 minutes.
5. Spoon 2 tablespoons pizza sauce onto each chicken breast, sprinkle each with half the mozzarella cheese, and top each with half the pepperoni slices.
6. Bake until chicken is no longer pink inside and the juices run clear, about 10 more minutes. An instant-read meat thermometer inserted into the thickest part of a breast should read at least 160 degrees F (70 degrees C).

CHANA MASALA (SAVORY INDIAN CHICK PEAS)
Servings: 2 | Prep: 15m | Cooks: 15m | Total: 30m

NUTRITION FACTS

Calories: 413.4 | Carbohydrates: 46.2g | Protein: 9.4g | Cholesterol: 0mg | Sodium: 524.9mg

INGREDIENTS

- 1 onion, chopped

- 1 tomato, chopped

- 1 (1 inch) piece fresh ginger, peeled and chopped

- 4 cloves garlic, chopped, or more to taste

- 1 green chile pepper, seeded and chopped

- 1 teaspoon coriander powder

- 1 teaspoon garam masala

- 1/2 teaspoon turmeric powder

- 1 pinch salt to taste

- 1 cup water as needed

- 3 tablespoons olive oil
- 2 bay leaves, or more to taste
- 1 teaspoon chili powder
- 1 (15 ounce) can chickpeas
- 1 teaspoon fresh cilantro leaves, for garnish, or more to taste

DIRECTIONS

1. Grind onion, tomato, ginger, garlic, and chile pepper together in a food processor into a paste.
2. Heat olive oil in a large skillet over medium heat. Fry bay leaves in hot oil until fragrant, about 30 seconds. Pour the paste into the skillet and cook until the oil begins to separate from the mixture and is golden brown in color, 2 to 3 minutes. Season the mixture with chili powder, coriander, powder, gram masala, turmeric, and salt; cook and stir until very hot, 2 to 3 minutes.
3. Stir enough water into the mixture to get a thick gravy; bring to a boil and stir chickpeas into the gravy. Reduce heat to medium and cook until the chickpeas are heated through, 5 to 7 minutes. Garnish with cilantro.

SPICY SALMON WITH CARAMELIZED ONIONS

Servings: 2 | Prep: 10m | Cooks: 10m | Total: 50m | Additional: 30m

NUTRITION FACTS

Calories: 495.7 | Carbohydrates: 11.3g | Protein: 29.5g | Cholesterol: 82.5mg | Sodium: 562.2mg

INGREDIENTS

- 1 1/2 teaspoons ground black pepper
- 1/2 teaspoon paprika
- 1/4 teaspoon cayenne pepper
- 1 teaspoon minced garlic
- 1 tablespoon Dijon mustard
- 1 tablespoon brown sugar
- 1/2 teaspoon onion powder
- 1/4 teaspoon salt
- 1 tablespoon olive oil
- 2 (6 ounce) salmon fillets
- 2 tablespoons olive oil
- 1 1/2 tablespoons minced onion

DIRECTIONS

1. Combine the black pepper, paprika, cayenne pepper, minced garlic, Dijon mustard, brown sugar, onion powder, and salt in a small bowl. Stir in 1 tablespoon of olive oil to make a paste. Spread the paste all over the salmon fillets, and set aside to marinate at room temperature 30 minutes.
2. Heat the remaining 2 tablespoons of olive oil in a small pan over medium heat. Stir in the onion, and cook until tender and golden brown, about 10 minutes. Heat a separate non-stick skillet over medium-high heat. Cook the salmon fillets in the hot skillet until golden brown on each side, and no longer translucent in the center, about 4 minutes per side. Pour the browned onions and olive oil over the salmon fillets to serve.

A PAD THAI WORTH MAKING

Servings: 3 | Prep: 15m | Cooks: 15m | Total: 30m

NUTRITION FACTS

Calories: 742.1 | Carbohydrates: 83.1g | Protein: 41.4g | Cholesterol: 280.2mg | Sodium: 1591.2mg

INGREDIENTS

- 1 (8 ounce) package dried flat rice noodles
- 3 tablespoons fish sauce
- 1/4 cup fresh lime juice
- 1 tablespoon white sugar
- 2 tablespoons oyster sauce
- 1 1/2 tablespoons Asian chile pepper sauce, divided
- 1/4 cup chicken stock
- 1/4 cup vegetable oil
- 1 tablespoon chopped garlic
- 8 ounces medium shrimp - peeled and deveined
- 8 ounces skinless, boneless chicken breast halves - cut into 1 inch cubes
- 2 eggs, beaten
- 3 cups bean sprouts
- 6 green onions, chopped into 1 inch pieces
- 2 tablespoons chopped unsalted dry-roasted peanuts
- 1/4 cup chopped fresh cilantro
- 1 lime, cut into 8 wedges
- 2 cups bean sprouts

DIRECTIONS

1. Fill a large bowl with hot tap water and place the noodles in it to soak for 20 minutes.

2. In a small bowl, stir together the fish sauce, lime juice, sugar, oyster sauce, 2 teaspoons of the chile sauce and chicken stock. Set aside.

3. Heat a wok or large skillet over high heat and add vegetable oil. When the oil is hot, stir in garlic and cook for about 10 seconds. Add shrimp and chicken; cook, stirring constantly until shrimp is opaque and chicken is cooked through, 5 to 7 minutes.

4. Move everything in the wok out to the sides and pour the eggs in the center. Cook and stir the eggs until firm. Add the noodles to the wok and pour in the sauce. Cook, stirring constantly, until the noodles are tender. Add a bit more water if needed to finish cooking the noodles. Stir in 3 cups of bean sprouts and green onions. Remove from the heat and garnish with chopped peanuts. Taste for seasoning, adjusting the spice or lime juice if needed.

5. Serve garnished with fresh cilantro and remaining bean sprouts and lime wedges on the side.

JALAPENO POPPER GRILLED CHEESE SANDWICH

Servings: 2 | Prep: 10m | Cooks: 10m | Total: 20m

NUTRITION FACTS

Calories: 528.1 | Carbohydrates: 40.9g | Protein: 16.5g | Cholesterol: 88.5mg | Sodium: 1120.6mg

INGREDIENTS

- 2 ounces cream cheese, softened
- 1 tablespoon sour cream
- 10 eaches pickled jalapeno pepper slices, or to taste - chopped
- 2 ciabatta sandwich rolls
- 4 teaspoons butter
- 8 eaches tortilla chips, crushed
- 1/2 cup shredded Colby-Monterey Jack cheese

DIRECTIONS

1. Combine the cream cheese, sour cream, and pickled jalapeno in a small bowl. Set aside. Preheat skillet over medium heat.

2. Slice each roll in half horizontally, then slice the rounded tops off the ciabatta rolls to make a flat top half. Spread 1 teaspoon butter on the doughy cut side of the bottom bun and 1 teaspoon butter on the now flattened top bun. Place half of the cream cheese mixture, half of the crushed chips, and half of the shredded cheese on the non-buttered side of the bottom bun. Place the top half of the bun on the sandwich and place the sandwich on the hot skillet. Repeat with the second sandwich.

3. Grill until lightly browned and flip over, about 3 to 5 minutes; continue grilling until cheese is melted and the second side is golden brown.

POTATO CAKE

Servings: 2 | Prep: 15m | Cooks: 20m | Total: 35m

NUTRITION FACTS

Calories: 602.7 | Carbohydrates: 61.6g | Protein: 24.5g | Cholesterol: 171.8mg | Sodium: 1226.3mg

INGREDIENTS

- 2 cups mashed potatoes
- 1 egg, beaten
- 1/2 cup all-purpose flour
- salt to taste
- 1 pinch garlic salt
- 1 tablespoon butter
- 1 cup shredded Cheddar cheese

DIRECTIONS

1. In a medium size mixing bowl combine mashed potatoes, egg, flour, salt (if needed) and garlic salt. Mix well.
2. Melt butter in a large frying pan over a low heat. Drop pancake-size (4 inch circles) lumps of mashed potatoes into the frying pan. Pat to flatten to 1/2 to 1 inch thickness. Sprinkle some cheddar cheese onto the mashed potato cake. Spoon more potato mixture over the cheese. Flip the potato cake over when the bottom is browned (about 10 minutes). Brown the other side (about 10 minutes).

STUFFED EGGPLANT WITH SHRIMP AND BASIL

Servings: 2 | Prep: 30m | Cooks: 45m | Total: 1h15m

NUTRITION FACTS

Calories: 923.9 | Carbohydrates: 59.1g | Protein: 22.6g | Cholesterol: 53.7mg | Sodium: 2380.3mg

INGREDIENTS

- 1 eggplant, halved lengthwise
- 1/2 cup olive oil, divided
- 1 teaspoon salt and pepper to taste
- 8 medium shrimp - peeled, deveined and chopped
- 2 cloves garlic, chopped
- 1/2 cup white wine
- 1 cup Italian seasoned bread crumbs
- 1/2 cup grated Parmesan cheese, divided

- 1/8 cup chopped fresh
  basil

DIRECTIONS

1. Preheat oven to 350 degrees F (175 degrees C). Scoop out the flesh of the eggplant, chop, and reserve. Coat shells with olive oil, and season with salt and pepper; set aside.
2. Heat 1/4 cup olive oil in a large, deep skillet over medium high heat. Saute shrimp, basil and garlic until shrimp turns pink, about 1 minute. Stir in the reserved chopped eggplant. Season with salt and pepper. Pour in wine, and cook 5 minutes.
3. Transfer to a large bowl, and mix in the bread crumbs and 1/4 cup Parmesan cheese. If mixture is dry, stir in more olive oil. Stuff mixture into eggplant shells, and sprinkle top with remaining Parmesan cheese.
4. Bake in preheated oven for 30 to 40 minutes, or until eggplant is tender.

CHICKEN SCALLOPINI

Servings: 2 | Prep: 20m | Cooks: 20m | Total: 40m

NUTRITION FACTS

Calories: 541.7 | Carbohydrates: 34.8g | Protein: 34.8g | Cholesterol: 128.2mg | Sodium: 884.4mg

INGREDIENTS

- 1 clove garlic, pressed
- 1/4 cup butter, softened
- 2 skinless, boneless chicken breast halves
- 1/2cup all-purpose flour
- 1 pinch salt and ground black pepper to taste
- 4 ounces sliced mushrooms
- 20 eaches capers, or to taste
- 2 tablespoons lemon juice
- 1/4 cup white wine
- 2 tablespoons chicken-flavored demi-glace, or to taste
- 1 teaspoon chopped fresh parsley, or to taste
- 2 lemon slices

DIRECTIONS

1. In a small bowl, stir together the garlic and butter until well combined. Set aside. Place a chicken breast half on a work surface with the thick side facing to the right (if you're right-handed), and place your left hand down on the chicken breast. Using a very sharp knife, carefully cut the chicken breast from the thick side to about 1/2 inch from the edge of the thin side, in a horizontal cut. Open the cut

chicken breast and spread it out like an open book. Using a meat mallet, gently pound the butterflied chicken breast out until it's an even thickness.

2. Place the flour into a shallow dish, and dredge each chicken breast on both sides with flour. Melt the garlic butter in a large skillet over medium heat until it stops foaming, and cook each chicken breast until golden brown on both sides, 6 to 8 minutes per side. Sprinkle each breast with salt and pepper. Remove the chicken breasts to a platter, and keep warm.

3. Cook and stir the mushrooms in the same skillet as the chicken until the mushrooms have absorbed the remaining butter in the skillet and have begun to turn brown at the edges. Stir in capers, lemon juice, white wine, and chicken demi-glace, and stir to combine. Reduce to a simmer. Adjust salt and pepper again, and stir the parsley into the sauce.

4. Remove the chicken breasts to plates, and serve the sauce over the chicken. Garnish each serving with a lemon slice.

DELICIOUS GRILLED HAMBURGERS

Servings: 3 | Prep: 5m | Cooks: 10m | Total: 15m

NUTRITION FACTS

Calories: 396.4 | Carbohydrates: 1.9g | Protein: 28.2g | Cholesterol: 98.7mg | Sodium: 21.7mg

INGREDIENTS

- 1 pound lean ground beef
- 1 tablespoon Worcestershire sauce
- 1 tablespoon liquid smoke flavoring
- 1 teaspoon garlic powder
- 1 tablespoon olive oil
- 1 pinch seasoned salt to taste

DIRECTIONS

1. Preheat a grill for high heat.
2. In a medium bowl, lightly mix together the ground beef, Worcestershire sauce, liquid smoke and garlic powder. Form into 3 patties, handling the meat minimally. Brush both sides of each patty with some oil, and season with seasoned salt.
3. Place the patties on the grill grate, and cook for about 5 minutes per side, until well done.

COLA ONION PORK CHOPS

Servings: 3 | Prep: 5m | Cooks: 1h | Total: 1h5m

NUTRITION FACTS

Calories: 235.2 | Carbohydrates: 18.7g | Protein: 22.2g | Cholesterol: 59.1mg | Sodium: 865.2mg

INGREDIENTS

- 3 thick cut boneless pork chops
- 1 (1 ounce) envelope dry onion soup mix
- 1 (12 fluid ounce) can cola-flavored carbonated beverage

DIRECTIONS

1. Preheat the oven to 350 degrees F (175 degrees C).
2. Place the pork chops in a shallow glass baking dish. Pour the cola over them, and sprinkle with onion soup mix.
3. Bake uncovered for 30 minutes in the preheated oven. Turn over, and continue baking for another 30 minutes, until sauce is thickened and chops are fork tender.

ALTERNATIVE BAKED SALMON

Servings: 2 | Prep: 15m | Cooks: 15m | Total: 30m

NUTRITION FACTS

Calories: 440.6 | Carbohydrates: 28.2g | Protein: 25.1g | Cholesterol: 60.5mg | Sodium: 688.6mg

INGREDIENTS

- 1 tablespoon olive oil
- 1 small yellow onion, chopped
- 1/2 teaspoon dried minced garlic
- salt and pepper to taste
- 1/2 cup herb seasoned bread crumbs
- 2 tablespoons mayonnaise, or as needed
- 1 teaspoon mustard powder
- 2 eaches salmon fillets (about 1 inch thick)

DIRECTIONS

1. Preheat the oven to 350 degrees F (175 degrees C). Grease a baking sheet, and set aside.
2. Heat oil in a skillet over medium-high heat. Saute onion with dried garlic, salt and pepper until tender. Transfer to a medium bowl, and mix with bread crumbs, mustard powder and mayonnaise. If necessary, add more mayonnaise to achieve a paste-like consistency.
3. Place salmon fillets onto the greased baking sheet, and press the crumb mixture on the top so that it is about 1/4 inch thick.
4. Bake for 10 minutes in the preheated oven, until salmon is easily cut with a fork, then broil for 5 minutes to crisp the top.

VEGETARIAN BIBIMBAP

Servings: 3 | Prep: 30m | Cooks: 20m | Total: 50m

NUTRITION FACTS

Calories: 395.2 | Carbohydrates: 45g | Protein: 13.6g | Cholesterol: 196.2mg | Sodium: 1085.8mg

INGREDIENTS

- 2 tablespoons sesame oil
- 1 cup carrot matchsticks
- 1 cup zucchini matchsticks
- 1/2 (14 ounce) can bean sprouts, drained
- 6 ounces canned bamboo shoots, drained
- 1 (4.5 ounce) can sliced mushrooms, drained
- 1/8 teaspoon salt to taste
- 2 cups cooked and cooled rice
- 1/3 cup sliced green onions
- 2 tablespoons soy sauce
- 1/4 teaspoon ground black pepper
- 1 tablespoon butter
- 3 eggs
- 3 teaspoons sweet red chili sauce, or to taste

DIRECTIONS

1. Heat sesame oil in a large skillet over medium heat; cook and stir carrot and zucchini in the hot oil until vegetables begin to soften, about 5 minutes. Stir in bean sprouts, bamboo shoots, and mushrooms. Cook and stir until carrots are tender, about 5 more minutes. Season to taste with salt and set vegetables aside.
2. Stir cooked rice, green onions, soy sauce, and black pepper in the same skillet until the rice is hot. In a separate skillet over medium heat, melt butter and gently fry eggs, turning once, until the yolks are still slightly runny but the egg whites are firm, about 3 minutes per egg.
3. To serve, divide hot cooked rice mixture between 3 serving bowls and top each bowl with 1/3 of the vegetable mixture and a fried egg. Serve sweet red chili sauce on the side for mixing into bibimbap.

PHYLLO-WRAPPED HALIBUT FILLETS WITH LEMON SCALLION SAUCE

Servings: 2 | Prep: 20m | Cooks: 15m | Total: 35m

NUTRITION FACTS

Calories: 587.3 | Carbohydrates: 24.7g | Protein: 33.9g | Cholesterol: 157.4mg | Sodium: 367.5mg

INGREDIENTS

- 2 tablespoons melted butter
- 4 sheets phyllo dough
- 2 (5 ounce) halibut fillets
- 1 pinch salt and pepper to taste
- 2 teaspoons chopped fresh dill
- 3 tablespoons lemon juice
- 1/2 cup whipping cream
- 2 green onions, finely chopped

DIRECTIONS

1. Preheat oven to 425 degrees F (220 degrees C).
2. Lightly butter 1 sheet of phyllo dough. Lay another sheet directly on top of the first sheet, and lightly butter it. Repeat with remaining 2 sheets of phyllo. Cut sheets in half.
3. Season halibut fillets with salt and pepper. Place a fillet near the bottom edge of one of the halved sheets of phyllo. Sprinkle with dill. Fold in the sides of the phyllo, then roll the fillet. Place on a baking sheet, and lightly brush with butter. Repeat with remaining fillet.
4. Bake in a preheated oven until pastry is puffed and golden brown, about 12 to 15 minutes.
5. Meanwhile, bring lemon juice to a boil in a small saucepan over high heat. Boil until almost evaporated. Reduce heat to medium, and stir in cream. Simmer until the cream thickens somewhat. Stir in green onions, and season with salt and pepper. Serve halibut on a pool of sauce.

GRILLED MONGOLIAN PORK CHOPS

Servings: 2 | Prep: 20m | Cooks: 40m | Total: 7h | Additional: 6h

NUTRITION FACTS

Calories: 839 | Carbohydrates: 62.1g | Fat: 47.4g | Protein: 41.8g | Cholesterol: 265mg

Sodium: 1960mg

INGREDIENTS

- 1/2 cup hoisin sauce
- 4 cloves garlic, minced
- 1 1/2 tablespoons soy sauce
- 1 tablespoon grated fresh ginger
- 1 tablespoon red wine vinegar
- 1/2 teaspoon freshly ground black pepper
- 2 (10 ounce) thick bone-in center cut pork chops
- 1/4 cup red wine vinegar
- 3 tablespoons white sugar
- 2 tablespoons hot mustard powder (such as Coleman's) or Chinese

style, to taste

- 1 tablespoon rice vinegar
- 1 tablespoon sherry vinegar
- 2 teaspoons sesame oil
- 2 teaspoons white sugar
- 1 1/2 teaspoons hot sauce
- 1/2 teaspoon ground white pepper
- 1 egg yolk
- 1/3 cup creme fraiche
- 1 teaspoon Dijon mustard
- 1/4 teaspoon ground turmeric
- cayenne pepper to taste

DIRECTIONS

1. Combine hoisin sauce, garlic, soy sauce, ginger, 1 tablespoon red wine vinegar, rice vinegar, sherry vinegar, sesame oil, 2 teaspoons sugar, hot sauce, white pepper, and black pepper in a large bowl. Whisk thoroughly and set aside.
2. Place pork chops in a resealable freezer bag; pour slightly more than 1/2 the marinade into freezer bag over pork chops. Seal bag and refrigerate for 6 to 8 hours. Reserve remaining marinade.
3. Combine 1/4 cup red wine vinegar, 3 tablespoons sugar, 2 tablespoons hot mustard powder, and egg yolk in a small saucepan over medium-low heat. Whisk until slightly thickened, about 5 minutes; remove from heat.
4. Stir in creme fraiche, Dijon mustard, turmeric, and cayenne pepper. Refrigerate until needed.
5. Remove pork chops from marinade and pat dry using paper towel.
6. Preheat an outdoor grill for high heat, and lightly oil the grate.
7. Cook pork chops on the preheated grill until browned grill marks appear, about 4 minutes per side.
8. Move pork chops from directly above heat source. Continue cooking over indirect medium heat, brushing the remaining marinade on each side, until no longer pink inside, about 25 minutes. An instant-read thermometer inserted into the center should read 145 degrees F (63 degrees C). Serve pork chops topped with mustard sauce.

FETA AND SUN-DRIED TOMATO STUFFED CHICKEN

Servings: 2 | Prep: 30m | Cooks: 30m | Total: 1h30m | Additional: 30m

NUTRITION FACTS

Calories: 838.2 | Carbohydrates: 15.7g | Protein: 45.6g | Cholesterol: 147.3mg | Sodium: 2641.8mg

INGREDIENTS

- 1/3 cup lemon juice
- 1 (4 ounce) package crumbled feta cheese

- 1/3 cup extra-virgin olive oil
- 2 tablespoons Greek seasoning
- 2 teaspoons lemon zest
- 2 (6 ounce) skinless, boneless chicken breast halves
- 6 chopped sun-dried tomatoes
- 10 eaches pitted and coarsely chopped kalamata olives
- 1 tablespoon oil from the sun-dried tomatoes
- 4 strips roasted red pepper

DIRECTIONS

1. Whisk together the lemon juice, extra-virgin olive oil, Greek seasoning, and lemon zest in a bowl. Pound the chicken breasts between sheets of wax paper or plastic wrap to a thickness of 1/4 inch. Marinate the chicken in the lemon marinade at least 30 minutes. Meanwhile, stir together the feta cheese, sun-dried tomatoes, kalamata olives, and 1 tablespoon of oil from the jar of sun-dried tomatoes in a small bowl; set aside.
2. Preheat oven to 375 degrees F (190 degrees C).
3. Remove the chicken from the marinade, and shake off excess. Discard the remaining marinade. Divide the stuffing mixture onto each piece of chicken. Fold the edges of the chicken over the filling, and secure with toothpicks. Place onto a baking dish, seam-side down, and place two roasted pepper strips onto each stuffed breast.
4. Bake in the preheated oven until the chicken is no longer pink, about 30 minutes. Remember to remove the toothpicks before serving.

LOBSTER TAILS STEAMED IN BEER

Servings: 2 | Prep: 5m | Cooks: 8m | Total: 13m

NUTRITION FACTS

Calories: 209.3 | Carbohydrates: 4.1g | Protein: 36.1g | Cholesterol: 180.5mg | Sodium: 566mg

INGREDIENTS

- 2 whole lobster tail
- 1/2 (12 fluid ounce) can beer

DIRECTIONS

1. In a medium saucepan, over medium to high heat, bring the beer to a boil.
2. If lobster tails are still in the shell, split the shell lengthwise first.
3. Place a steamer basket on top of the saucepan. place thawed lobster tails in basket and cover. Reduce heat and simmer for 8 minutes.

BAKED TOFU

Servings: 2 | Prep: 15m | Cooks: 1h | Total: 1h15m

NUTRITION FACTS

Calories: 332.1 | Carbohydrates: 23.2g | Protein: 20.3g | Cholesterol: 0mg | Sodium: 919.1mg

INGREDIENTS

- 1 pound tofu, sliced into 8 even pieces
- 2 tablespoons soy sauce
- 2 tablespoons agave nectar
- 1 tablespoon toasted sesame oil
- 1 teaspoon minced garlic
- 1 teaspoon minced fresh ginger
- 1 tablespoon sesame seeds, or to taste

DIRECTIONS

1. Preheat oven to 350 degrees F (175 degrees C). Lightly oil a large baking sheet.
2. Gently press tofu pieces to release as much water as possible. Arrange tofu on the prepared baking sheet.
3. Whisk soy sauce, agave nectar, sesame oil, garlic, and ginger together in a bowl until marinade is evenly combined. Brush half of the marinade over tofu pieces.
4. Bake in the preheated oven for 30 minutes. Flip tofu and brush remaining marinade over tofu. Sprinkle sesame seeds over tofu. Continue baking until tofu is crisp, about 30 minutes more. Transfer tofu to a wire rack using a spatula; cool.

LONDON BROIL

Servings: 3 | Prep: 10m | Cooks: 10m | Total: 4h20m | Additional: 4h

NUTRITION FACTS

Calories: 487.1 | Carbohydrates: 2.4g | Protein: 44.6g | Cholesterol: 112.8mg | Sodium: 1192.3mg

INGREDIENTS

- 1 1/2 pounds top round, London Broil cut
- 1 tablespoon meat tenderizer
- 1/3 cup vegetable oil
- 1/4 teaspoon lemon pepper
- 2 cloves garlic, minced
- 4 teaspoons chopped fresh parsley

- 2 teaspoons lemon juice
- 2 teaspoons seasoning salt
- 2 teaspoons tarragon vinegar

DIRECTIONS

1. Score top and bottom of meat with a 1 1/2 inch square pattern, and score the side. Sprinkle meat liberally with unseasoned meat tenderizer, then pierce with fork 1/8 inch apart and at least half-way through the meat on both sides. Sprinkle lightly with water, and rub in tenderizer. Place on a plate, cover, and set aside for an hour.
2. In a small bowl, mix together oil, lemon juice, seasoned salt, lemon pepper, garlic, parsley, and tarragon vinegar. Pour marinade over meat, reserving a portion to be used for brushing (Note: DO NOT mix the reserved marinade with the meat; set aside for later). Pour remaining marinade over meat, recover dish and refrigerate for three hours, turning every half hour.
3. Preheat grill for hot heat.
4. Lightly oil grate, and position it 2 inches above the coals. Place meat on grill, and cook for 5 minutes. Turn meat over, brush with marinade, and cook for another 5 minutes.

HONEY SOY TILAPIA

Servings: 2 | Prep: 10m | Cooks: 15m | Total: 55m | Additional: 30m

NUTRITION FACTS

Calories: 217.7 | Carbohydrates: 33.3g | Protein: 19.4g | Cholesterol: 31mg | Sodium: 1398.7mg

INGREDIENTS

- 3 tablespoons honey
- 3 tablespoons soy sauce
- 3 tablespoons balsamic vinegar
- 1 tablespoon minced garlic
- 2 (3 ounce) fillets tilapia
- 1 serving cooking spray
- 1 teaspoon freshly cracked black pepper

DIRECTIONS

1. Mix the honey, soy sauce, balsamic vinegar, and garlic together in a bowl. Place the tilapia fillets in the mixture; allow to marinate in refrigerator at least 30 minutes.
2. Preheat an oven to 350 degrees F (175 degrees C). Spray a baking dish with cooking spray.

3. Remove tilapia from marinade, and discard the marinade. Place fillets into the prepared baking sheet, and sprinkle the black pepper over the fish.
4. Bake in the preheated oven until the fish flakes easily with a fork, 15 to 20 minutes.

ACCIDENTAL FISH

Servings: 2 | Prep: 10m | Cooks: 20m | Total: 30m

NUTRITION FACTS

Calories: 556 | Carbohydrates: 3g | Protein: 21.7g | Cholesterol: 203.8mg | Sodium: 451.6mg

INGREDIENTS

- 2 (4 ounce) fillets mahi mahi
- 2 teaspoons olive oil
- 1/2 cup salted butter
- 1 clove garlic, minced
- 1 tablespoon lemon juice
- 2 drops Louisiana-style hot sauce, or to taste
- 1 roma tomato, seeded and chopped
- 1 green onion, chopped

DIRECTIONS

1. Preheat an oven to 450 degrees F (230 degrees C).
2. Rub the mahi mahi fillets with the olive oil and lay into a baking dish.
3. Bake in the preheated oven until the fish flakes easily with a fork, about 20 minutes.
4. While the mahi mahi bakes, melt the butter in a saucepan over medium heat.
5. Stir the garlic, lemon juice, and hot sauce into the melted butter; simmer together for 1 minute. Add the tomato and green onion to the butter mixture; cook and stir until hot. Spoon over the baked fish to serve.

STIR-FRY PORK WITH GINGER

Servings: 2 | Prep: 15m | Cooks: 15m | Total: 30m

NUTRITION FACTS

Calories: 321.7 | Carbohydrates: 2.2g | Protein: 9.4g | Cholesterol: 40.9mg | Sodium: 837.6mg

INGREDIENTS

- 2 tablespoons vegetable oil
- 1/2 teaspoon salt

- 1/2 inch piece fresh ginger root, thinly sliced
- 1/4 pound thinly sliced lean pork
- 1 teaspoon soy sauce
- 1/2 teaspoon dark soy sauce
- 1/3 teaspoon sugar
- 1 teaspoon sesame oil
- 1 green onion, chopped
- 1 tablespoon Chinese rice wine

DIRECTIONS

1. Heat oil in a large skillet or wok over medium-high heat. Fry ginger in hot oil until fragrant, then add pork, soy sauce, dark soy sauce, salt, and sugar. Cook, stirring occasionally, for 10 minutes.
2. Stir in the sesame oil, green onion, and rice wine. Simmer until the pork is tender.

ORANGE, HONEY AND SOY CHICKEN

Servings: 2 | Prep: 15m | Cooks: 20m | Total: 35m

NUTRITION FACTS

Calories: 320 | Carbohydrates: 46.3g | Protein: 25.7g | Cholesterol: 60.8mg | Sodium: 2112.1mg

INGREDIENTS

- 2 skinless, boneless chicken breast halves, diced
- 2 fruit (2-3/8" dia)s oranges, juiced
- 1/4 cup soy sauce
- 1/4 cup honey
- 1 tablespoon garlic paste
- 1 tablespoon ginger paste
- 1 pinch ground black pepper to taste

DIRECTIONS

1. Combine chicken, orange juice, soy sauce, honey, garlic paste, ginger paste, and black pepper in a large nonstick skillet over medium-high heat. Cook and stir until the sauce reduces to a sticky glaze and the chicken is cooked through, about 20 minutes.

CHICKEN MASSAMAN CURRY

Servings: 4 | Prep: 20m | Cooks: 35m | Total: 55m

NUTRITION FACTS

Calories: 689.6 | Carbohydrates: 47.3g | Protein: 38.1g | Cholesterol: 73.3mg | Sodium: 1220.7mg

INGREDIENTS

- 2 tablespoons vegetable oil
- 3 tablespoons curry paste
- 1 (3/4 inch thick) slice ginger, minced
- 1 1/4 pounds skinless, boneless chicken breast meat - cubed
- 3 tablespoons brown sugar
- 3 tablespoons fish sauce
- 3 tablespoons tamarind paste
- 1/3 cup peanut butter
- 3 cups peeled, cubed potatoes
- 1 (13.5 ounce) can coconut milk
- 3 tablespoons fresh lime juice

DIRECTIONS

1. Heat vegetable oil in a large saucepan over medium heat. Stir in curry paste and minced ginger; cook and stir for 2 minutes. Stir in the cubed chicken, and cook until the pieces turn white on the outside, about 3 minutes.
2. Stir in brown sugar, fish sauce, tamarind paste, peanut butter, potatoes, and coconut milk. Bring to a boil, then reduce heat to medium-low, cover, and simmer until the potatoes are tender and the chicken pieces are no longer pink in the center, about 20 minutes. Add the lime juice and cook for an additional 5 minutes before serving.

LEMON GARLIC CHICKEN

Servings: 3 | Prep: 10m | Cooks: 15m | Total: 25m

NUTRITION FACTS

Calories: 214.4 | Carbohydrates: 4.7g | Protein: 24.7g | Cholesterol: 85mg | Sodium: 1275.4mg

INGREDIENTS

- 2 tablespoons butter
- 3 eaches skinless, boneless chicken breast
- 1 1/2 teaspoons ground black pepper
- 2 tablespoons garlic powder

halves

- 1 1/2 teaspoons salt
- 1 lemon, juiced

DIRECTIONS

1. Melt butter in a skillet over medium-high heat.
2. Season chicken with salt and pepper; place in the melted butter. Cook chicken, flipping frequently, until browned, about 5 minutes. Sprinkle 1 tablespoon garlic powder over chicken; flip and sprinkle 1 tablespoon garlic powder on second side. Cook each side for 2 minutes.
3. Pour lemon juice over each side of chicken and cook until no longer pink in the center, 5 to 10 minutes more. An instant-read thermometer inserted into the center should read at least 165 degrees F (74 degrees C).

STIR-FRY PORK WITH GINGER

Servings: 2 | Prep: 15m | Cooks: 15m | Total: 30m

NUTRITION FACTS

Calories: 321.7 | Carbohydrates: 2.2g | Protein: 9.4g | Cholesterol: 40.9mg | Sodium: 837.6mg

INGREDIENTS

- 2 tablespoons vegetable oil
- 1/2 inch piece fresh ginger root, thinly sliced
- 1/4 pound thinly sliced lean pork
- 1 teaspoon soy sauce
- 1/2 teaspoon dark soy sauce
- 1/2 teaspoon salt
- 1/3 teaspoon sugar
- 1 teaspoon sesame oil
- 1 green onion, chopped
- 1 tablespoon Chinese rice wine

DIRECTIONS

1. Heat oil in a large skillet or wok over medium-high heat. Fry ginger in hot oil until fragrant, then add pork, soy sauce, dark soy sauce, salt, and sugar. Cook, stirring occasionally, for 10 minutes.
2. Stir in the sesame oil, green onion, and rice wine. Simmer until the pork is tender.

LIME-MARINATED MAHI MAHI

Servings: 2 | Prep: 10m | Cooks: 10m | Total: 35m | Additional: 15m

NUTRITION FACTS

Calories: 860 | Carbohydrates: 2.5g | Protein: 21g | Cholesterol: 81.8mg | Sodium: 99.4mg

INGREDIENTS

- 3/4 cup extra-virgin olive oil
- 1 clove garlic, minced
- 1/8 teaspoon ground black pepper
- 1/2 teaspoon cayenne pepper
- 1 pinch salt
- 2 tablespoons lime juice
- 1/8 teaspoon grated lime zest
- 2 (4 ounce) mahi mahi fillets
- 2 twists lime zest

DIRECTIONS

1. Preheat an outdoor grill for medium heat, and lightly oil the grate.
2. Whisk the extra-virgin olive oil, minced garlic, black pepper, cayenne pepper, salt, lime juice, and grated lime zest together in a bowl to make the marinade.
3. Place the mahi mahi fillets in the marinade and turn to coat; allow to marinate at least 15 minutes.
4. Cook on the preheated grill until the fish flakes easily with a fork and is lightly browned, 3 to 4 minutes per side.
5. Garnish with the twists of lime zest to serve.

SAUTEED SCALLOPS

Servings: 2 | Prep: 5m | Cooks: 5m | Total: 10m

NUTRITION FACTS

Calories: 408.6 | Carbohydrates: 6.5g | Protein: 38.5g | Cholesterol: 135.9mg

INGREDIENTS

- 1/4 cup butter
- 2 sprigs fresh rosemary
- 2 cloves crushed garlic
- 1 pound scallops

DIRECTIONS

1. In a medium size saucepan melt butter over medium-high heat. Add crushed garlic and whole sprigs of rosemary to the saucepan. Add scallops, cook for 2 minutes on each side (or until desired consistency). Remove the garlic and rosemary from pan. Serve.

WILD RICE AND ASPARAGUS CHICKEN BREASTS

Servings: 2 | Prep: 20m | Cooks: 10m | Total: 30m

NUTRITION FACTS

Calories: 635.4 | Carbohydrates: 56.6g | Protein: 37.1g | Cholesterol: 69.2mg | Sodium: 473.4mg

INGREDIENTS

- 1 whole boneless, skinless chicken breast, cubed
- 2 cups wild rice, cooked
- 1/2 pound fresh asparagus
- 3 tablespoons hoisin sauce
- 4 tablespoons peanut oil
- 1 tablespoon brown sugar

DIRECTIONS

1. Cut asparagus into 3/4 inch to 1 inch pieces, discarding tough bottoms of spears. In a small bowl, mix together the hoisin sauce and brown sugar and set aside. Prepare rice OR reheat cooked rice and keep warm.
2. Heat wok over medium high heat. When hot, dribble 1 tablespoon of oil around the rim. Stir fry asparagus for approximately 2 minutes. Remove from the wok and keep warm. Heat wok to high heat.
3. Heat wok to high heat. Add 2 tablespoons of oil and the chicken pieces and stir fry until the chicken is no longer pink. Add the reserved asparagus and hoisin/sugar sauce and stir fry all together until pieces are coated with sauce. Serve over the hot rice.

SLOPPY JOE SANDWICHES

Servings: 2 | Prep: 5m | Cooks: 40m | Total: 45m

NUTRITION FACTS

Calories: 466.8 | Carbohydrates: 47.8g | Protein: 24g | Cholesterol: 69.4mg | Sodium: 1339.4mg

INGREDIENTS

- 1/2 pound ground beef
- 1/2 onion, chopped
- 1/2 cup ketchup
- 2 tablespoons water
- 1 tablespoon brown sugar
- 1 teaspoon Worcestershire sauce
- 1 teaspoon prepared mustard
- 1 teaspoon white vinegar
- 1 teaspoon chili powder
- 1/4teaspoon garlic powder
- 1/4teaspoon onion powder
- 1/4 teaspoon salt
- 2 hamburger buns, split

DIRECTIONS

1. Heat a large skillet over medium-high heat and stir in ground beef and onion. Cook and stir until beef is crumbly, evenly browned, and no longer pink, about 10 minutes. Drain and discard any excess grease. Stir in ketchup, water, brown sugar, Worcestershire sauce, mustard, vinegar, chili powder, garlic powder, onion powder, and salt.
2. Bring beef mixture to a boil over high heat. Reduce heat to low; cover and simmer until sauce has thickened, 30 to 40 minutes. Serve on buns.

PAN-POACHED ALASKAN SALMON PICCATA

Servings: 2 | Prep: 5m | Cooks: 25m | Total: 30m

NUTRITION FACTS

Calories: 262.3 | Carbohydrates: 1.8g | Protein: 22.7g | Cholesterol: 81.3mg

INGREDIENTS

- 1/2 cup water
- 2 tablespoons lemon juice
- 1/8 teaspoon chicken bouillon granules
- 2 (4 ounce) fillets salmon
- 1 tablespoon butter
- 2 tablespoons capers
- ground black pepper to taste
- 1 tablespoon chopped fresh parsley

DIRECTIONS

1. Bring water and lemon juice to a boil in medium-sized skillet. Stir in chicken bouillon granules. Reduce heat to a simmer and place salmon fillets in pan. Cover and simmer over low heat, 10 minutes per inch of thickness, measured at thickest part; or until fish flakes when tested with a fork. Remove salmon from pan; keep salmon warm.
2. Boil remaining liquid in the skillet until it is reduced to approximately 1/4 cup. Whisk in butter and stir in capers. Spoon sauce over fish. Season with pepper and sprinkle with parsley.

TENDER TOMATO CHICKEN BREASTS

Servings: 3 | Prep: 10m | Cooks: 35m | Total: 45m

NUTRITION FACTS

Calories: 325.5 | Carbohydrates: 36.2g | Protein: 30g | Cholesterol: 64.1mg | Sodium: 1301.9mg

INGREDIENTS

- 1 tablespoon olive oil
- 3 skinless, boneless chicken breast halves
- 1 tablespoon ground black pepper, or to taste
- 3 tablespoons onion powder, or to taste
- 1 (28 ounce) can chopped stewed tomatoes, 1/2 the liquid reserved
- 1 (14 ounce) can chicken broth
- 1 (10 ounce) package frozen mixed vegetables
- 1/4 cup water

DIRECTIONS

1. Heat the oil in a skillet over medium heat. Season chicken breasts on both sides with pepper and onion powder, and arrange in the skillet. Cook 2 minutes on each side, just until browned. Pour tomatoes and reserved liquid over the chicken. Pour in broth. Cover skillet, and continue cooking 15 minutes on each side, until chicken juices run clear.
2. While the chicken is cooking, place the frozen mixed vegetables and water in a pot. Scoop about 3/4 cup liquid from the skillet, and mix into the pot. Bring to a boil, and cook 5 minutes, or until vegetables are tender; drain. Arrange chicken breasts over the vegetables, and drizzle with liquid from the skillet to serve.

FRENCH EGG AND BACON SANDWICH

Servings: 2 | Prep: 5m | Cooks: 15m | Total: 20m

NUTRITION FACTS

Calories: 738 | Carbohydrates: 79.3g | Protein: 22.9g | Cholesterol: 410.1mg | Sodium: 954.1mg

INGREDIENTS

- 2 eggs, beaten
- 4 slices bacon
- 1/2 cup maple syrup
- 4 slices bread
- 2 eggs

DIRECTIONS

1. Dip bread slices in beaten eggs. Heat a lightly oiled griddle or frying pan over medium high heat. Cook until browned on both sides. Set aside but keep warm.
2. Place bacon in a large, deep skillet. Cook over medium high heat until evenly brown. Drain and set aside. Reserve 1 tablespoon of bacon grease in pan and fry remaining two eggs.
3. Place one piece of French toast on each of two plates. Place the fried eggs on top of the bread, top the eggs with strips of bacon. Cover with the remaining pieces of French toast. Following that by pouring on the syrup.

STIR-FRY CHICKEN AND VEGETABLES

Servings: 2 | Prep: 20m | Cooks: 20m | Total: 40m

NUTRITION FACTS

Calories: 313.8 | Carbohydrates: 20.2g | Protein: 22.1g | Cholesterol: 45.4mg | Sodium: 1265mg

INGREDIENTS

- 6 ounces skinless, boneless chicken breast, cut into small pieces
- 2 tablespoons soy sauce
- 2 tablespoons dry sherry
- 1 tablespoon cornstarch
- 1 tablespoon vegetable oil
- 1 large green bell pepper, cut into squares
- 1 zucchini, cut into rounds and quartered
- 3 cloves garlic, minced
- 1/2 cup chicken broth
- 1 tablespoon vegetable oil

- 1 cup broccoli florets, cut into pieces
- 6 eaches green onions, chopped

DIRECTIONS

1. Mix chicken, soy sauce, sherry, and cornstarch in a bowl.
2. Heat 1 tablespoon vegetable oil in a large skillet or wok over medium-high heat; cook and stir broccoli, bell pepper, zucchini, and garlic for 2 to 3 minutes. Add chicken broth, cover, and simmer until vegetables are tender, 4 to 5 minutes. Transfer vegetables and sauce to a large bowl and wipe skillet clean.
3. Heat remaining 1 tablespoon vegetable oil over medium-high heat; cook and stir chicken until meat is no longer pink in the center, about 5 minutes. Stir in vegetables; continue to cook and stir for 2 to 3 minutes more. Sprinkle with green onions.

LOW CARB PANCAKE CREPES

Servings: 2 | Prep: 5m | Cooks: 20m | Total: 25m

NUTRITION FACTS

Calories: 240.7 | Carbohydrates: 2.4g | Protein: 9.6g | Cholesterol: 238.2mg | Sodium: 215.4mg

INGREDIENTS

- 3 ounces cream cheese, softened
- 1 teaspoon ground cinnamon
- 1 teaspoon butter
- 2 eggs, beaten
- 1 tablespoon sugar-free syrup

DIRECTIONS

1. In a bowl, mash the cream cheese with beaten eggs, about 1 teaspoon at a time at first, until the mixture is smooth and free of lumps. Beat in the cinnamon and sugar-free syrup.
2. Melt the butter in a nonstick skillet over medium heat. When the butter has stopped foaming, reduce heat to medium-low, and pour in several tablespoons of the batter. Swirl to coat the bottom of the skillet. Allow to cook until set, about 4 minutes on the first side; flip the crepe with a spatula and cook the other side until the crepe shows small browned spots, 1 to 2 more minutes.

BROWN SUGAR HAM STEAK

Servings: 2 | Prep: 10m | Cooks: 15m | Total: 25m

NUTRITION FACTS

Calories: 521 | Carbohydrates: 33.3g | Protein: 22.4g | Cholesterol: 127.2mg | Sodium: 1647.9mg

INGREDIENTS

- 1 (8 ounce) bone-in fully cooked ham steak
- 5 tablespoons brown sugar
- 5 tablespoons butter, cubed

DIRECTIONS

1. Cook ham steak in a large skillet over medium heat until browned, 3 to 4 minutes per side. Drain and remove ham.
2. Heat butter in the same skillet until melted; stir in brown sugar. Return ham to skillet and cook over medium-low heat until heated through and brown sugar is dissolved, turning steak often, about 10 minutes.

SPICY GRILLED CHEESE SANDWICH

Servings: 2 | Prep: 2m | Cooks: 3m | Total: 5m

NUTRITION FACTS

Calories: 352.3 | Carbohydrates: 28.2g | Protein: 10.7g | Cholesterol: 57.2mg | Sodium: 846.4mg

INGREDIENTS

- 2 tablespoons butter or margarine
- 4 slices white bread
- 2 slices American cheese
- 1 roma (plum) tomato, thinly sliced
- 1/4 small onion, chopped
- 1 jalapeno pepper, chopped

DIRECTIONS

1. Heat a large skillet over low heat. Spread butter or margarine onto one side of two slices of bread. Place both pieces buttered side down in the skillet. Lay a slice of cheese on each one, and top with slices of tomato, onion and jalapeno. Butter one side of the remaining slices of bread, and place on

top buttered side up. When the bottom of the sandwiches are toasted, flip and fry until brown on the other side.

ONE-DISH ROCKFISH

Servings: 2 | Prep: 20m | Cooks: 20m | Total: 40m

NUTRITION FACTS

Calories: 233.4 | Carbohydrates: 11.5g | Protein: 35.5g | Cholesterol: 63.7mg | Sodium: 417.2mg

INGREDIENTS

- 5 cups fresh spinach
- 2 (6 ounce) fillets rockfish
- 10 eaches cherry tomatoes, halved
- 1/2 cup vegetable broth
- 2 tablespoons minced fresh dill
- 1/4 teaspoon garlic powder
- 1/2 teaspoon lemon pepper
- 1/2 teaspoon onion powder
- 1 pinch salt and ground black pepper to taste
- 2 slices lemon slices
- 2 slices onion slices
- 1 teaspoon butter

DIRECTIONS

1. Preheat oven to 400 degrees F (200 degrees C).
2. Layer the spinach in the bottom of a 2 quart baking dish. Lay the rockfish atop the spinach. Scatter the tomatoes around the fish. Pour the broth into the dish. Season the fillet with the dill, garlic powder, lemon pepper, onion powder, salt, and pepper. Place the lemon, onion, and butter on the rockfish. Cover the entire dish with aluminum foil.
3. Bake in preheated oven until the fish flakes easily, 20 to 25 minutes.

QUICK EGGPLANT PARMESAN

Servings: 2 | Prep: 5m | Cooks: 10m | Total: 15m

NUTRITION FACTS

Calories: 644 | Carbohydrates: 63.6g | Protein: 36.5g | Cholesterol: 167.2mg | Sodium: 1865.7mg

INGREDIENTS

- 1 egg
- 1 1/2 cups shredded mozzarella cheese

- 1 tablespoon water
- 1 small eggplant, cut into 3/4 inch thick slices
- 1 cup dried bread crumbs, seasoned
- 1/4 cup spaghetti sauce
- 1/4 teaspoon crushed red pepper flakes
- 3 tablespoons grated Parmesan cheese

DIRECTIONS

1. In a small bowl beat the egg and water together. Place the bread crumbs in shallow dish. Dip eggplant slices in egg mixture then in crumbs, being sure to coat thoroughly.
2. Heat oil in a large skillet over medium-high heat until hot. Add eggplant slices and reduce heat to medium. Cook for 3 to 4 minutes per side or until golden brown and tender. Sprinkle mozzarella cheese over eggplant during last minute of cooking to melt.
3. While eggplant is cooking, combine spaghetti sauce and pepper flakes in a microwave-safe measuring cup. Cover with plastic wrap and cook at high power for 2 minutes or until heated through.
4. Top eggplant with sauce and Parmesan cheese and serve.

RILLED SALMON WITH BACON AND CORN RELISH

Servings: 2 | Prep:20m | Cooks: 25m | Total: 45m

NUTRITION FACTS

Calories: 605 | Carbohydrates: 20.2g | Fat: 33.1g | Protein: 56.6g | Cholesterol: 141mg | Sodium: 755mg

INGREDIENTS

- G6 slices bacon, cut crosswise into 1/2-inch pieces
- 2 ears white corn
- 1/4 cup chopped green onions - white and light green parts separated from green tops
- 1/4 cup diced red bell pepper
- salt and ground black pepper to taste
- 1 pinch cayenne pepper, or to taste
- 2 teaspoons olive oil
- 1 tablespoon rice vinegar, or more to taste
- 1/2 teaspoon vegetable oil
- 2 (8 ounce) center-cut boneless salmon fillets
- 1 pinch cayenne pepper, or to taste
- 1 cup fresh spinach leaves (optional)

DIRECTIONS

1. Preheat an outdoor grill (preferably charcoal) for high heat and lightly oil the grate.
2. Place bacon in a skillet over medium heat and cook until browned and crisp, 8 to 10 minutes.
3. Cut kernels from corn ears into a large bowl using a sharp knife held at a 45-degree angle. Scrape cobs with the back of the knife into the bowl to get the juices.
4. Stir white and light green parts of green onions into bacon and add red bell pepper; cook and stir until vegetables just start to become tender, about 2 minutes. Stir corn into bacon mixture and let corn just warm through. Season with salt, black pepper, cayenne pepper, a few chopped dark green onion tops, olive oil, and rice vinegar. Turn off heat under relish.
5. Spread vegetable oil onto both sides of salmon fillets and season fish with salt, black pepper, and cayenne pepper.
6. Cook on preheated grill until fish shows good grill marks, the flesh flakes easily, and fish is still slightly pink in the center, about 5 minutes per side. A crack that opens up in the salmon flesh as you cook will let you see how done the salmon is in the middle.
7. Divide spinach leaves onto 2 plates and top each with a salmon fillet and half the bacon relish. Sprinkle on a few green onion tops for garnish.

TROUT AMANDINE

Servings: 2 | Prep: 15m | Cooks: 20m | Total: 35m

NUTRITION FACTS

Calories: 854 | Carbohydrates: 24.4g | Protein: 66.4g | Cholesterol: 223.5mg | Sodium: 315.3mg

INGREDIENTS

- 2 whole (10 ounce) trout, pan-dressed
- salt and pepper to taste
- 1/4 cup all-purpose flour
- 4 tablespoons butter
- 1/2 cup blanched slivered almonds
- 2 tablespoons lemon juice
- 1 tablespoon chopped fresh parsley, for garnish
- 8 slices lemon, for garnish

DIRECTIONS

1. Rinse and pat dry trout. Season inside and out with salt and pepper to taste. Dredge trout in flour.
2. Heat 2 tablespoons butter in large skillet over high heat until melted. Add trout and brown both sides. Lower heat to medium and cook for about 5 minutes on each side or until cooked through. Remove trout to a serving plate and keep warm.
3. Wipe out pan and add 2 tablespoons butter. Cook butter over medium heat until it just begins to brown. Add the almonds and brown.

4. Pour sauce and almonds over fish and sprinkle with lemon juice and parsley. Garnish with fresh lemon slices.

MINUTE STEAKS WITH BARBEQUE BUTTER SAUCE

Servings: 2 | Prep: 5m | Cooks: 2m | Total: 7m

NUTRITION FACTS

Calories: 318 | Carbohydrates: 4.6g | Fat: 22g | Protein: 24.1g | Cholesterol: 81mg | Sodium: 409mg

INGREDIENTS

- 2 (5 ounce) boneless sirloin steaks
- salt and freshly ground black pepper to taste
- 1/2 cup beef broth
- 1 1/2 tablespoons barbeque sauce
- 1 dash hot pepper sauce
- freshly ground black pepper
- 1 teaspoon cold butter, or more to taste
- 1 tablespoon vegetable oil

DIRECTIONS

1. Place each steak between two sheets of heavy plastic (or inside a resealable freezer bag) on a solid, level surface. Firmly pound each steak with the smooth side of a meat mallet to a thickness of 1/4-inch. Remove steaks from plastic.
2. Generously season each steak with salt and ground black pepper. Set aside.
3. Combine beef broth, barbeque sauce, hot sauce, and black pepper in a bowl. Add chilled butter to broth mixture but do not stir.
4. Heat oil in a large skillet over high heat until it just begins to smoke, about 1 minute. Place each steak in the pan; sear for 45 to 60 seconds on each side. Remove steaks from skillet and set them aside to rest.
5. Pour the broth mixture into the skillet and bring to a boil while scraping the browned bits of food off of the bottom of the pan with a wooden spoon. Stir occasionally until butter is melted and incorporated, about 2 minutes.
6. Spoon broth and butter mixture over steak and serve.

KETO CHICKEN PARMESAN

Servings: 2 | Prep: 20m | Cooks: 8m | Total: 28m

NUTRITION FACTS

Calories: 441.5 | Carbohydrates: 5.8g | Protein: 46.5g | Cholesterol: 216.8mg | Sodium: 1604.7mg

INGREDIENTS

- 1 (8 ounce) skinless, boneless chicken breast
- 1 egg
- 1 tablespoon heavy whipping cream
- 1 1/2 ounces pork rinds, crushed
- 1 ounce grated Parmesan cheese
- 1/2 teaspoon salt
- 1/2 teaspoon garlic powder
- 1/2 teaspoon red pepper flakes
- 1/2 teaspoon ground black pepper
- 1/2 teaspoon Italian seasoning
- 1/2 cup jarred tomato sauce (such as Rao's)
- 1/4 cup shredded mozzarella cheese
- 1 tablespoon ghee (clarified butter)
- 1/2 teaspoon red pepper flakes

DIRECTIONS

1. Set oven rack about 6 inches from the heat source and preheat the oven's broiler.
2. Slice chicken breast through the middle horizontally from one side to within 1/2 inch of the other side. Open the two sides and spread them out like an open book. Pound chicken flat until about 1/2-inch thick.
3. Beat egg and cream together in a bowl.
4. Combine crushed pork rinds, Parmesan cheese, salt, garlic powder, red pepper flakes, ground black pepper, and Italian seasoning in bowl; transfer breading to a plate.
5. Dip chicken into egg mixture; coat completely. Press chicken into breading; thickly coat both sides.
6. Heat a skillet over medium-high heat; add ghee. Place chicken in the pan; cook until no longer pink in the center and the juices run clear, about 3 minutes per side. An instant-read thermometer inserted into the center should read at least 165 degrees F (74 degrees C). Be careful to keep breading in place.
7. Transfer chicken to a baking sheet. Cover with tomato sauce; top with mozzarella cheese.
8. Broil until cheese is bubbling and barely browned, about 2 minutes.

SEAFOOD SANDWICH

Servings: 2 | Prep: 15m | Cooks: 5m | Total: 50m | Additional: 30m

NUTRITION FACTS

Calories: 478 | Carbohydrates: 39.7g | Protein: 13g | Cholesterol: 48.1mg | Sodium: 1413.3mg

INGREDIENTS

- 1 (8 ounce) package imitation crab or lobster
- 1/4 teaspoon OLD BAY Seasoning

meat

- 1/4 cup mayonnaise
- 1 tablespoon finely chopped red onion
- 1 teaspoon lemon juice
- 1 tablespoon butter, softened
- 2 hot dog buns

DIRECTIONS

1. In a medium bowl, flake the crabmeat, and mix in mayonnaise, onion, lemon juice and Old Bay seasoning. Cover and refrigerate for 30 minutes to allow the flavors to mingle.
2. Spread butter on the inside of the hot dog buns, and toast under the broiler. Fill buns with the crab salad, and serve.

LEMON GARLIC SALMON

Servings: 2 | Prep: 5m | Cooks: 25m | Total: 30m

NUTRITION FACTS

Calories: 323 | Carbohydrates: 6.9g | Protein: 23.3g | Cholesterol: 96.6mg | Sodium: 300.6mg

INGREDIENTS

- 2 tablespoons unsalted butter
- 2 teaspoons minced garlic
- 1 teaspoon lemon pepper
- 2 (4 ounce) fillets salmon
- 1 lemon

DIRECTIONS

1. Season salmon fillets on both sides with lemon pepper.
2. In a large skillet, melt butter over medium high heat. Stir in garlic. Place salmon in pan. Cook for 10 minutes per inch of thickness, or until fish flakes when tested with a fork. Flip fillets halfway through cooking to brown on both sides. Sprinkle with lemon juice before serving.

GREEK COUSCOUS

Servings: 3 | Prep: 20m | Cooks: 5m | Total: 45m

NUTRITION FACTS

Calories: 254 | Carbohydrates: 42.4g | Fat: 5.6g | Protein: 9g | Cholesterol: 6mg

INGREDIENTS

- 1/4 cup chicken broth
- 1/2 cup water
- 1 teaspoon minced garlic
- 1/2 cup pearl (Israeli) couscous
- 1/4 cup chopped sun-dried tomatoes
- 1/4 cup sliced Kalamata olives
- 2 tablespoons crumbled feta cheese
- 1 cup canned garbanzo beans, rinsed and drained
- 1 teaspoon dried oregano
- 1/2 teaspoon ground black pepper
- 1 tablespoon white wine vinegar
- 1 1/2 teaspoons lemon juice

DIRECTIONS

1. Pour the chicken broth and water into a saucepan, stir in the garlic, and bring to a boil. Stir in the couscous, cover the pan, and remove from heat. Allow the couscous to stand until all the water has been absorbed, about 5 minutes; fluff with a fork. Allow the couscous to cool to warm temperature.
2. In a large serving bowl, lightly toss the couscous, sun-dried tomatoes, olives, feta cheese, and garbanzo beans. Mix the oregano, black pepper, white wine vinegar, and lemon juice in a small bowl, and pour over the couscous mixture. Toss again to serve.

SASSY STEAK MARINADE AND SAUCE

Servings: 2 | Prep: 10m | Cooks: 20m | Total: 1h | Additional: 30m

NUTRITION FACTS

Calories: 728.4 | Carbohydrates: 62.1g | Protein: 42.9g | Cholesterol: 121mg | Sodium: 2690.4mg

INGREDIENTS

- 1 pound beef sirloin steaks
- 1 tablespoon olive oil
- 3 cloves garlic, crushed
- 1/4 teaspoon seasoning salt, or to taste

- 2/3 cup cocktail sauce
- 1/4 cup honey
- 3 tablespoons soy sauce
- 1 tablespoon olive oil
- 8 ounces sliced fresh mushrooms

DIRECTIONS

1. Pierce steaks all over with a fork, and place them into a resealable freezer bag. In a medium bowl, stir together 1 tablespoon of olive oil, cocktail sauce, honey, soy sauce, garlic, and seasoning salt. Pour over the steaks in the bag, seal, and refrigerate for 30 minutes or up to 6 hours, turning frequently.
2. Preheat an outdoor grill for medium-high heat. When grill is heated, lightly oil the grate.
3. Remove steaks from marinade, reserving marinade. Grill for about 7 minutes on each side, or to your desired degree of doneness.
4. While steaks are grilling, heat the remaining tablespoon of olive oil in a skillet over medium heat. Add mushrooms, and cook until tender. Pour in reserved marinade, and bring to a boil. Boil for 5 minutes, or until thickened. Serve with steaks.

CHINESE SPARERIBS

Servings: 2 | Prep: 5m | Cooks: 40m | Total: 2h45m | Additional: 2h

NUTRITION FACTS

Calories: 502.8 | Carbohydrates: 23g | Protein: 30.4g | Cholesterol: 120.5mg | Sodium: 1014.9mg

INGREDIENTS

- 3 tablespoons hoisin sauce
- 1 tablespoon ketchup
- 1 tablespoon honey
- 1 tablespoon soy sauce
- 1 tablespoon sake
- 1 teaspoon rice vinegar
- 1 teaspoon lemon juice
- 1 teaspoon grated fresh ginger
- 1/2 teaspoon grated fresh garlic
- 1/4 teaspoon Chinese five-spice powder
- 1 pound pork spareribs

DIRECTIONS

1. In a shallow glass dish, mix together the hoisin sauce, ketchup, honey, soy sauce, sake, rice vinegar, lemon juice, ginger, garlic and five-spice powder. Place the ribs in the dish, and turn to coat. Cover and marinate in the refrigerator for 2 hours, or as long as overnight.
2. Preheat the oven to 325 degrees F (165 degrees C). Fill a broiler tray with enough water to cover the bottom. Place the grate or rack over the tray. Arrange the ribs on the grate.
3. Place the broiler rack in the center of the oven. Cook for 40 minutes, turning and brushing with the marinade every 10 minutes. Let the marinade cook on for the final 10 minutes to make a glaze. Finish under the broiler if desired. Discard any remaining marinade.

MEDITERRANEAN TILAPIA

Servings: 2 | Prep: 10m | Cooks: 15m | Total: 25m

NUTRITION FACTS

Calories: 183.5 | Carbohydrates: 5.4g | Protein: 24g | Cholesterol: 41.4mg | Sodium: 464mg

INGREDIENTS

- 3 tablespoons sun-dried tomatoes packed in oil, drained and chopped
- 1 tablespoon capers, drained
- 2 eaches tilapia fillets
- 1 tablespoon oil from the jar of sun-dried tomatoes
- 1 tablespoon lemon juice
- 2 tablespoons kalamata olives, pitted and chopped

DIRECTIONS

1. Preheat the oven to 375 degrees F (190 degrees C). In a small bowl, stir together the sun-dried tomatoes, olives and capers. Set aside.
2. Place the tilapia fillets side by side in a baking dish. Drizzle with oil and lemon juice.
3. Bake for 10 to 15 minutes in the preheated oven, until the fish flakes with a fork. Check after 10 minutes, so as not to overcook, or the fish may be dry. When fish is done, top with the tomato mixture, and serve.

SALMON IN PARCHMENT

Servings: 2 | Prep: 10m | Cooks: 40m | Total: 55m

NUTRITION FACTS

Calories: 873 | Carbohydrates: 114.7g | Fat: 18.5g | Protein: 62.7g | Cholesterol: 100mg

Sodium: 114.7mg

INGREDIENTS

- 1 teaspoon olive oil, or more if needed
- 6 small potatoes
- 10 spears asparagus
- 2 (8 ounce) skinless, boneless, center-cut salmon fillets
- salt and ground black pepper to taste
- 1 teaspoon extra-virgin olive oil

DIRECTIONS

1. Preheat oven to 400 degrees F (200 degrees C).
2. Take two pieces of parchment paper, fold in half, and cut a half-circle starting at each crease. They should look similar to a heart-shape when unfolded. Coat each piece of parchment with olive oil on both sides.
3. Place potatoes in a saucepan and cover with salted water; bring to a boil. Reduce heat to medium-low and simmer until tender, about 20 minutes. Drain.
4. Bring a pot of lightly salted water to a boil. Add asparagus, and cook uncovered until slightly tender, about 5 minutes. Drain in a colander, then immediately immerse in ice water for several minutes until cold to stop the cooking process. Once the asparagus is cold, drain well, and set aside.
5. Place 1 salmon fillet, half the asparagus, and half the potatoes in the middle of one side of a prepared parchment paper. Sprinkle with salt and pepper and drizzle with extra-virgin olive oil. Fold other half of circle over and seal parchment edge by making overlapping folds around the edge. At the end, fold the last crease in the opposite direction of the rest to ensure it seals. Repeat with the second piece of prepared parchment and remaining ingredients. Place pouches on a baking sheet.
6. Bake in the preheated oven for 15 minutes. Remove from oven and allow to sit for 5 minutes before cutting open parchment. The salmon is done when it flakes easily with a fork.

PASTA MELANZANA

Servings: 4 | Prep: 10m | Cooks: 15m | Total: 25m

NUTRITION FACTS

Calories: 296.7 | Carbohydrates: 16.6g | Protein: 10.5g | Cholesterol: 24.1mg | Sodium: 329mg

INGREDIENTS

- 3/4 cup bow tie (farfalle) pasta
- 1 medium eggplant, peeled and cubed
- 4 tablespoons olive oil
- 4 cloves garlic, finely chopped
- 1 tablespoon butter
- 3 cups fresh spinach, chopped
- 3 tablespoons fresh lemon juice
- 1 pinch salt and pepper
- 3/4 cup grated Parmesan cheese, divided
- 1 pinch cracked black pepper to taste

DIRECTIONS

1. Bring a large pot of lightly salted water to a boil. Add pasta and cook for 8 to 10 minutes or until al dente; drain. Keep warm.
2. Meanwhile, heat the olive oil and butter in a skillet over medium heat. Add the garlic; cook and stir until softened. Mix in the eggplant. Let the eggplant cook for 5 minutes without stirring. Then stir and cook until tender, about 5 more minutes
3. Mix in the spinach and season with salt, and pepper. Cook, stirring occasionally, for 3 minutes. Stir in the drained pasta and lemon juice along with 1/2 cup Parmesan cheese. Transfer to a serving dish and top with remaining cheese and cracked black pepper.

HOW TO COOK TROUT

Servings: 2 | Prep: 15m | Cooks: 10m | Total: 25m

NUTRITION FACTS

Calories: 470 | Carbohydrates: 1.6g | Fat: 33.2g | Protein: 40.4g | Cholesterol: 181mg | Sodium: 263mg

INGREDIENTS

- 1/4 cup butter
- 2 (8 ounce) whole trout, butterflied and deboned
- salt and freshly ground black pepper to taste
- 2 tablespoons freshly squeezed lemon juice
- 2 tablespoons chopped fresh flat-leaf parsley

DIRECTIONS

1. Melt butter in a saucepan over medium-low heat until butter smells toasted and is golden brown, about 1 minute. Turn off heat.

2. Line a baking sheet with a piece of aluminum foil. Place trout onto foil; open trout so skin sides are down. Drizzle each trout with about 1/2 teaspoon melted butter. Generously season with salt and black pepper.
3. Move an oven rack to 5 or 6 inches below heat source and preheat oven's broiler on high heat.
4. Broil trout until opaque and barely firm to the touch, 2 or 3 minutes. Remove from oven.
5. Return pan of melted butter over high heat; stir in lemon juice and parsley. Bring butter sauce to a boil; whisk to combine. Serve trout on plates and drizzle with butter sauce.

BLUEBERRY LEMON BREAKFAST QUINOA

Servings: 2 | Prep: 5m | Cooks: 25m | Total: 30m

NUTRITION FACTS

Calories: 538 | Carbohydrates: 98.7g | Fat: 7.3g | Protein: 21.5g | Cholesterol: 5mg | Sodium: 112mg

INGREDIENTS

- 1 cup quinoa
- 2 cups nonfat milk
- 1 pinch salt
- 3 tablespoons maple syrup
- 1/2 lemon, zested
- 1 cup blueberries
- 2 teaspoons flax seed

DIRECTIONS

1. Rinse quinoa in a fine strainer with cold water to remove bitterness until water runs clear and is no longer frothy.
2. Heat milk in a saucepan over medium heat until warm, 2 to 3 minutes. Stir quinoa and salt into the milk; simmer over medium-low heat until much of the liquid has been absorbed, about 20 minutes. Remove saucepan from heat. Stir maple syrup and lemon zest into the quinoa mixture. Gently fold blueberries into the mixture
3. Divide quinoa mixture between 2 bowls; top each with 1 teaspoon flax seed to serve.

MALAYSIAN MANGO CHICKEN CURRY

Servings: 2 | Prep: 20m | Cooks: 20m | Total: 40m

NUTRITION FACTS

Calories: 360.9 | Carbohydrates: 42g | Protein: 29g | Cholesterol: 66.1mg | Sodium: 707.9mg

INGREDIENTS

- 1 tablespoon vegetable oil
- 1/2 pound skinless, boneless chicken breast, cubed
- 1/2 cup chicken stock
- 1 tablespoon soy sauce
- 1 tablespoon cider vinegar
- 1 1/2 tablespoons brown sugar
- 1 teaspoon curry powder
- 1 tablespoon cornstarch
- 1/2 onion, diced
- 1 green bell pepper, sliced
- 1 red bell pepper, sliced
- 2 teaspoons minced fresh ginger root
- 1 mango, peeled and cubed

DIRECTIONS

1. Heat vegetable oil in a large skillet over medium-high heat and stir in the chicken breast. Cook the chicken breast until no longer pink in the center. Transfer cooked chicken to a plate. Meanwhile, whisk together the chicken stock, soy sauce, vinegar, brown sugar, curry powder, and cornstarch. Set aside.
2. Using the same skillet, cook and stir the onion over medium heat until the onion has softened and turned translucent, about 5 minutes. Stir in the green and red bell peppers and cook for 2 minutes, then add the ginger and cook for another minute. Stir in the chicken stock mixture and the cooked chicken breast. Cook until the sauce has thickened. Drop mango in and cook until the mango is heated through.

SOUTHERN FRIED CATFISH

Servings: 2 | Prep: 20m | Cooks: 10m | Total: 30m

NUTRITION FACTS | Sodium: mg

Calories: 1427.2 | Carbohydrates: 131.6g | Protein: 45.7g | Cholesterol: 145mg | Sodium: 799.9mg

INGREDIENTS

- 1/2 cup buttermilk
- 1/2 cup water
- 1 pinch salt and pepper, to taste
- 1 1/2 cups fine cornmeal
- 1/2 cup all-purpose flour
- 1 teaspoon seafood seasoning, such as Old Bay™

- 1 pound catfish fillets, cut in strips
- 1 quart vegetable oil for deep frying

DIRECTIONS

1. In a small bowl, mix buttermilk, water, salt, and pepper. Pour mixture into a flat pan large enough to hold the fillets. Spread fish in one layer over bottom of pan, turning to coat each side, and set aside to marinate.
2. In a 2 gallon resealable plastic bag, combine the cornmeal, flour, and seafood seasoning. Add fish to mixture, a few fillets at a time, and tumble gently to coat evenly.
3. Heat oil in deep fryer to 365 degrees F (185 degrees C).
4. Deep fry fillets until golden brown, about 3 minutes. Avoid overcrowding so fillets have room to brown properly. Fish should be slightly crisp outside, and moist and flaky inside. Drain on paper towels.

JOEL'S JERK CHICKEN PINEAPPLE PASTA

Servings: 2 | Prep: 15m | Cooks: 25m | Total: 40m

NUTRITION FACTS

Calories: 627.8 | Carbohydrates: 79.2g | Protein: 35.1g | Cholesterol: 69.2mg | Sodium: 297.8mg

INGREDIENTS

- 1 tablespoon olive oil
- 2 eaches skinless, boneless chicken breast halves - cubed
- 1 (8 ounce) can pineapple tidbits with juice
- 1/4 cup shredded coconut
- 2 tablespoons brown sugar
- 1 teaspoon jerk seasoning mix
- 1/2teaspoon ground cinnamon
- 1/2teaspoon chili powder
- 1/2 teaspoon crushed red pepper flakes
- 1 pinch salt and ground black pepper to taste
- 4 ounces dry fettuccini noodles

DIRECTIONS

1. Heat olive oil in a skillet over medium heat. Cook and stir chicken until no longer pink and juices run clear, 7 to 10 minutes. Stir in the pineapple and its juice, coconut, brown sugar, jerk seasoning, cinnamon, chili powder, red pepper flakes, salt and pepper. Reduce heat to low and simmer 15 minutes.

2. Bring a large pot of lightly salted water to a boil. Add pasta and cook until al dente, 8 to 10 minutes; drain. Toss chicken mixture with drained pasta.

ASHLEY'S CHICKEN KATSU WITH TONKATSU SAUCE

Servings: 2 | Prep: 20m | Cooks: 10m | Total: 30m

NUTRITION FACTS

Calories: 718.3 | Carbohydrates: 73.1g | Protein: 30.2g | Cholesterol: 136.5mg | Sodium: 2290.2mg

INGREDIENTS

- 1/2 cup Worcestershire sauce
- 1/4 cup ketchup
- 2 tablespoons soy sauce
- 1 pinch pepper to taste
- 2 cups vegetable oil, for deep-fat frying
- 1/2 cup all-purpose flour
- 1/2 cup panko bread crumbs
- 1 pinch salt and pepper to taste
- 1 egg, beaten
- 2 skinless, boneless chicken breast halves - pounded to 1/4 inch thickness
- 1 green onion, thinly sliced

DIRECTIONS

1. For the sauce, stir together the Worcestershire sauce, ketchup, and soy sauce, and a pinch of pepper to taste. Set aside.
2. Heat oil in deep-fryer to 350 degrees F (175 degrees C).
3. Place flour and panko bread crumbs onto separate plates and season with salt and pepper. Place the beaten egg in a medium bowl. Dip flattened chicken pieces first into flour, then egg, and lastly bread crumbs.
4. Fry breaded chicken breasts in preheated oil until golden brown and no longer pink in center, about 8 minutes. Transfer to a paper towel-lined plate to absorb excess oil. Slice chicken into thin strips and top with a drizzle of sauce and a sprinkling of sliced green onions. Serve remaining sauce on the side for dipping.

BBQ TUNA FRITTERS

Servings: 2 | Prep: 5m | Cooks: 20m | Total: 25m

NUTRITION FACTS

Calories: 370.6 | Carbohydrates: 27.9g | Protein: 22.9g | Cholesterol: 111.9mg | Sodium: 440.2mg

INGREDIENTS

- 1 (5 ounce) can light tuna in water, drained
- 1 egg
- 2/3 cup quick-cooking oats
- 3 tablespoons barbeque sauce
- 3 tablespoons chopped green onion
- 1/2 teaspoon hot pepper sauce, or to taste
- 1/2 teaspoon dried savory
- 1 pinch salt
- 2 tablespoons vegetable oil

DIRECTIONS

1. In a medium bowl, stir together the tuna, egg and oats until blended. Mix in the barbeque sauce, green onion, hot pepper sauce, savory, and salt.
2. Heat the oil in a large skillet over medium heat. Spoon tablespoonfuls of the tuna mixture into the pan, and flatten slightly. Smaller patties hold together better. Cook until browned on each side, about 3 minutes per side.

JUICY BUTT STEAKS

Servings: 2 | Prep: 10m | Cooks: 4h | Total: 4h10m

NUTRITION FACTS

Calories: 764.4 | Carbohydrates: 68.4g | Protein: 45.5g | Cholesterol: 161.9mg | Sodium: 2820.6mg

INGREDIENTS

- 2 raw steak with refuse, 300 g; yields excluding refuses pork shoulder (Boston butt) steaks
- 1 large onion, sliced
- 2 cups ketchup
- 2 cups water
- 1 pinch salt and pepper to taste
- 1 teaspoon garlic powder, or to taste

DIRECTIONS

1. Heat a large skillet over medium heat. Season the pork steaks on both sides with salt, pepper and garlic powder. Place in the skillet and cook until browned on each side, about 4 minutes per side.
2. Place sliced onions on top of the steaks in the pan. Stir together the ketchup and water in a medium bowl; pour over the steaks. Bring to a simmer, then reduce the heat to medium-low, cover and cook for about 2 hours. The longer you cook, the better the meat tastes.

STICKY GARLIC PORK CHOPS

Servings: 2 | Prep: 10m | Cooks: 20m | Total: 1h30m | Additional: 1h

NUTRITION FACTS

Calories: 500 | Carbohydrates: 42.4g | Fat: 21g | Protein: 35g | Cholesterol: 90mg

INGREDIENTS

- 1/3 cup light brown sugar
- 6 cloves garlic, crushed, or more to taste
- 1/4 cup rice vinegar
- 2 tablespoons fish sauce
- 1 tablespoon soy sauce
- 1 tablespoon ketchup
- 1/2 teaspoon freshly ground black pepper
- 2 teaspoons hot sauce, or to taste
- 2 (10 ounce) thick-cut bone-in pork chops
- 1 teaspoon vegetable oil

DIRECTIONS

1. Combine brown sugar, garlic, rice vinegar, and fish sauce in a bowl for the marinade. Add a splash of soy sauce and a plop of ketchup. Finish off with black pepper and hot sauce.
2. Pour 1/2 of the marinade into a baking dish and lay pork chops over marinade. Pour the remaining marinade on top and toss pork chops until well coated. Wrap with plastic wrap and marinate in the refrigerator, flipping chops every 30 minutes, 1 to 2 hours.
3. Remove chops to a plate, scraping any excess marinade back into the baking dish.
4. Heat oil in a nonstick skillet over medium heat. Place chops in the hot oil. Cook until outsides are nicely charred and meat springs back when lightly prodded, about 5 minutes per side. Remove chops to a plate to rest.
5. Pour the marinade into the skillet. Raise heat to medium-high. Cook until marinade is reduced and sticky, 3 to 5 minutes. Return pork chops and any accumulated juices to the skillet.
6. Reduce heat to medium-low. Cook pork chops, flipping and basting occasionally, until the centers are slightly pink and sauce is to your desired degree of stickiness, 6 to 8 minutes. An instant-read

thermometer inserted into the thickest part of the pork should read about 145 degrees F (63 degrees C).

7. Plate each pork chop and spoon a portion of the sticky garlic sauce on top.

BLACK BEAN BREAKFAST BOWL

Servings: 2 | Prep: 10m | Cooks: 5m | Total: 15m

NUTRITION FACTS

Calories: 625.3 | Carbohydrates: 46.6g | Protein: 27.9g | Cholesterol: 372mg | Sodium: 1157.6mg

INGREDIENTS

- 2 tablespoons olive oil
- 4 eggs, beaten
- 1 (15 ounce) can black beans, drained and rinsed
- 1 avocado, peeled and sliced
- 1/4 cup salsa
- 1 pinch salt and ground black pepper to taste

DIRECTIONS

1. Heat olive oil in a small pan over medium heat. Cook and stir eggs until eggs are set, 3 to 5 minutes.
2. Place black beans in a microwave-safe bowl. Heat on High in the microwave until warm, about 1 minute.
3. Divide warmed black beans between two bowls.
4. Top each bowl with scrambled eggs, avocado, and salsa. Season with salt and black pepper.

SALSA BISCUIT CHICKEN

Servings: 3 | Prep: 20m | Cooks: 10m | Total: 30m

NUTRITION FACTS

Calories: 826.9 | Carbohydrates: 59g | Protein: 51g | Cholesterol: 141.1mg | Sodium: 2172.6mg

INGREDIENTS

- 3 skinless, boneless chicken breast halves
- 1 onion, chopped
- 1 cup salsa
- 2 cups shredded Cheddar cheese
- 1 (12 ounce) can refrigerated biscuit dough

DIRECTIONS

1. Preheat oven to 350 degrees F (175 degrees C). Bring a saucepan of lightly salted water to a boil. Add chicken breasts, and boil until easily shredded, about 20 minutes.
2. Saute onion in a medium saucepan until soft. Remove from heat and stir in salsa, then stir in cheese until melted. Add chicken and mix all together.
3. Roll out biscuits individually, adding a little of the chicken mixture to each one; then roll up, secure with toothpicks and place on a lightly greased cookie sheet.
4. Bake at 350 degrees F (175 degrees C) for about 10 minutes, or until biscuits are golden and hot.

PROSCIUTTO-WRAPPED CHERRY-STUFFED CHICKEN BREASTS

Servings: 2 | Prep: 20m | Cooks: 35m | Total: 1h5m | Additional: 10m

NUTRITION FACTS

Calories: 582.6 | Carbohydrates: 30.5g | Protein: 44.4g | Cholesterol: 230.4mg | Sodium: 566.7mg

INGREDIENTS

- PROSCIUTTO-WRAPPED CHERRY-STUFFED CHICKEN BREASTS
- 1 tablespoon vegetable oil
- 1/3 cup dried cherries, chopped
- 1/4 cup plain bread crumbs
- 1 egg yolk
- 1 1/2 tablespoons finely grated Parmigiano-Reggiano cheese
- 2 teaspoons olive oil
- 1 teaspoon fresh thyme
- 1 teaspoon fresh oregano, minced
- 2 cloves garlic, minced
- 1 pinch salt and pepper to taste
- 1 pinch cayenne pepper
- 2 (6 ounce) skinless, boneless chicken breast halves
- 4 thin slices prosciutto
- 3/4 cup chicken broth
- 1 1/2 tablespoons balsamic vinegar
- 1 tablespoon butter
- 1 pinch salt and pepper to taste

DIRECTIONS

1. Preheat the oven to 400 degrees F (200 degrees C).
2. Brush the inside of an oven-proof skillet with vegetable oil. Set aside.
3. Mix cherries, bread crumbs, egg yolk, Parmigiano-Reggiano cheese, olive oil, thyme, oregano, garlic, salt, black pepper, and cayenne pepper until combined.
4. Cut a 1-inch slit in each chicken breast by slicing at an angle from the thick end of the breast toward the thinner end.
5. Open flap and place one butterflied chicken breast between two sheets of heavy plastic (resealable freezer bags work well) on a solid, level surface. Firmly pound chicken with the smooth side of a meat mallet to a thickness of 1/2-inch. Repeat with the other breast.
6. Place half the stuffing on each chicken breast, place each breast on a piece of plastic wrap and roll into a tight roll, twisting the ends of the plastic wrap to hold create a tight package.
7. On a piece of plastic wrap, slightly overlap 2 slices of prosciutto so they are as wide as the rolled chicken breast. Unwrap rolled chicken breast and place the breast at one end of the prosciutto. Roll prosciutto around the stuffed breast using the plastic to make a tight roll. Repeat with the second stuffed breast and remaining 2 slices of prosciutto.
8. Lay 4 pieces of string on the cutting board, about 1-inch apart. Place chicken roll across the strings, and tie each into a knot to keep the chicken from unrolling. Repeat for the second stuffed breast.
9. Place stuffed, rolled chicken breasts in the prepared skillet and bake in the preheated oven until the prosciutto is browned and crispy and chicken is no longer pink, about 25 minutes. An instant-read thermometer inserted into the center should read at least 165 degrees F (74 degrees C). Remove chicken to a plate and loosely cover with aluminum foil.
10. Drain grease from the pan as desired, leaving juice and browned bits. Pour in chicken stock and balsamic vinegar, and bring to a boil over high heat. Cook, while scraping the browned bits from the bottom of the pan, until liquid has reduced by half, 5 to 6 minutes. Remove from heat, add butter and stir until melted. Season with salt and black pepper to taste.
11. Remove twine from chicken breasts; slice into bite-sized pieces. Serve drizzled with pan sauce.

ALOHA CHICKEN BURGERS

Servings: 2 | Prep: 20m | Cooks: 30m | Total: 1h20m | Additional: 30m

NUTRITION FACTS

Calories: 668 | Carbohydrates: 40.7g | Protein: 45.8g | Cholesterol: 128.6mg | Sodium: 3972mg

INGREDIENTS

- 2 skinless, boneless chicken breast halves
- 1/4 cup soy sauce
- 3 slices thick cut bacon
- 2 slices Swiss cheese
- 2 tablespoons mayonnaise
- 2 slices pineapple

- 2 eaches large hamburger buns, split
- 1 tablespoon softened butter
- 1/4 cup teriyaki sauce
- 2 slices tomato
- 2 slices of iceberg lettuce

DIRECTIONS

1. Place chicken breasts into a plastic zipper bag with soy sauce, seal the bag, and marinate in refrigerator for 30 minutes. While chicken is marinating, place the bacon in a large, deep skillet, and cook over medium-high heat, turning occasionally, until evenly browned, about 10 minutes. Drain the bacon slices on a paper towel-lined plate, and set aside. Spread cut sides of hamburger buns with butter.
2. Preheat an outdoor grill for medium heat, and lightly oil the grate.
3. Remove the chicken from the soy sauce, and discard the excess soy sauce. Place the chicken breasts onto the preheated grill, and grill until chicken shows good grill marks, is no longer pink inside, and the juices run clear, 4 to 5 minutes per side. When chicken is almost done, brush each piece generously on both sides with teriyaki sauce to finish grilling. Place a slice of Swiss cheese on each chicken breast, and cover with a lid to help the cheese melt onto the chicken.
4. While chicken is grilling, spread the buns open on the grill and cook until toasted and showing grill lines, about 2 minutes. Set the buns aside.
5. To assemble, spread the grilled sides of each bun with mayonnaise, and top each bottom bun with a cooked chicken breast, 1 1/2 slices of bacon, a slice of pineapple, a slice from a head of lettuce, a slice of tomato, and the top bun.

DAN'S FAVORITE CHICKEN SANDWICH

Servings: 2 | Prep: 15m | Cooks: 35m | Total: 50m

NUTRITION FACTS

Calories: 1062.7 | Carbohydrates: 84.8g | Protein: 59.8g | Cholesterol: 143.2mg | Sodium: 1663.5mg

INGREDIENTS

- 2 skinless, boneless chicken breast halves
- 2 tablespoons barbeque sauce
- 4 slices bacon
- 2 eaches hoagie rolls, split lengthwise
- 2 tablespoons Ranch dressing
- 4 slices Swiss cheese
- 1 small avocado - peeled, pitted and diced

DIRECTIONS

1. Preheat oven to 375 degrees F (190 degrees C). Coat a baking dish with cooking spray. Brush both sides of each chicken breast with barbeque sauce and place in the baking dish. Top each breast with 2 slices bacon.
2. Bake chicken 25 minutes in the preheated oven, until juices run clear. Drain bacon strips on paper towels, and slice breasts in half lengthwise.
3. Heat the oven broiler. Spread both halves of each hoagie roll with Ranch dressing. Place 2 breast halves on one half of each roll. Place 2 strips of bacon on each remaining roll half. Top each half with 1 slice Swiss cheese.
4. Arrange sandwich halves on the baking sheet, and broil 2 to 5 minutes, until the cheese is melted and bubbly. Layer chicken halves of sandwiches with avocado slices, and top with bacon halves to serve.

ROASTED VEGGIE PASTA

Servings: 3 | Prep: 15m | Cooks: 15m | Total: 30m

NUTRITION FACTS

Calories: 456.5 | Carbohydrates: 66.7g | Protein: 16.8g | Cholesterol: 6.2mg | Sodium: 213.1mg

INGREDIENTS

- 1/4 pound fresh asparagus
- 2 red bell pepper, sliced
- 1/4 pound crimini mushrooms, sliced
- 10 cloves roasted garlic, chopped
- 1/2 tomato, quartered
- 1/2 teaspoon chopped fresh rosemary
- 1/2 teaspoon chopped fresh oregano
- 2 tablespoons olive oil
- 8 ounces dry fettuccini noodles
- 1/4 cup grated Parmesan cheese
- 2 tablespoons tapenade

DIRECTIONS

1. Preheat oven to 350 degrees F (175 degrees C). Prepare asparagus by trimming woody base and cutting diagonally into 4 inch pieces.
2. In a roasting pan, combine asparagus, bell pepper, mushrooms, roasted garlic and tomato. Sprinkle with rosemary and oregano, then drizzle with olive oil. Bake in preheated oven for 15 minutes.
3. Bring a large pot of lightly salted water to a boil. Add pasta and cook for 8 to 10 minutes or until al dente; drain. Toss with Parmesan cheese, tapenade and roasted vegetables.

EASY SPICY MEXICAN-AMERICAN CHICKEN

Servings: 2 | Prep: 5m | Cooks: 40m | Total: 45m

NUTRITION FACTS

Calories: 427.1 | Carbohydrates: 11.1g | Protein: 39.3g | Cholesterol: 141.8mg | Sodium: 1610.2mg

INGREDIENTS

- 1/4 cup Mexican-style hot sauce (such as Valentina)
- 1 tablespoon paprika
- 1 tablespoon cayenne pepper
- 1 tablespoon brown sugar, or more to taste
- 4 eaches chicken thighs

DIRECTIONS

1. Preheat oven to 400 degrees F (200 degrees C). Grease a small baking dish.
2. Mix the hot sauce, paprika, ground cayenne pepper, and brown sugar in a bowl, and stir until the mixture is well combined. Place the chicken thighs in the baking dish, and coat them with a layer of sauce. Cover the dish with foil.
3. Bake in the preheated oven for 20 minutes. Remove the foil, and bake until the chicken has cooked through, and the sauce has thickened and started to brown, about 20 more minutes.

VERMICELLI NOODLE BOWL

Servings: 2 | Prep: 35m | Cooks: 25m | Total: 1h

NUTRITION FACTS

Calories: 658.7 | Carbohydrates: 112.3g | Protein: 26.2g | Cholesterol: 36.1mg | Sodium: 2565.2mg

INGREDIENTS

- 1/4 cup white vinegar
- 1/4 cup fish sauce
- 2 tablespoons white sugar
- 2 tablespoons lime juice
- 1 clove garlic, minced
- 1/4 teaspoon red pepper flakes
- 1 (8 ounce) package rice vermicelli noodles
- 1 cup finely chopped lettuce
- 1 cup bean sprouts
- 1 English cucumber, cut into 2-inch matchsticks
- 1/4 cup finely chopped pickled carrots
- 1/4 cup finely chopped diakon radish

- 1/2 teaspoon canola oil
- 2 tablespoons chopped shallots
- 2 eaches skewers
- 8 medium shrimp, with shells
- 3 tablespoons chopped cilantro
- 3 tablespoons finely chopped Thai basil
- 3 tablespoons chopped fresh mint
- 1/4 cup crushed peanuts

DIRECTIONS

1. Whisk together vinegar, fish sauce, sugar, lime juice, garlic, and red pepper flakes in small bowl. Set the sauce aside.
2. Heat vegetable oil a small skillet over medium heat. Add shallots; cook and stir and softened and lightly caramelized, about 8 minutes.
3. Preheat an outdoor grill for medium heat and lightly oil the grate. Skewer 4 shrimp on each skewer and grill until they turn pink and are charred on the outside, 1 to 2 minutes per side. Set aside.
4. Bring a large pot of water to a boil. Add vermicelli noodles and cook until softened, 12 minutes. Drain noodles and rinse with cold water, stirring to separate the noodles.
5. Assemble the vermicelli bowl by placing the cooked noodles in one half of each serving bowl and the lettuce and bean sprouts in the other half. Top each bowl with cucumbers, carrots, daikon, cilantro, Thai basil, mint, peanuts, and the caramelized shallots. Serve with shrimp skewers on top and sauce on the side. Pour sauce over the top and toss thoroughly to coat before eating.

ASIAN CARRYOUT NOODLES

Servings: 2 | Prep: 20m | Cooks: 30m | Total: 50m

NUTRITION FACTS

Calories: 498.8 | Carbohydrates: 75.4g | Protein: 28.1g | Cholesterol: 34.6mg | Sodium: 1257mg

INGREDIENTS

- 1 (8 ounce) package angel hair pasta
- 1 teaspoon canola oil
- 1 teaspoon sesame oil
- 1/2 onion, chopped
- 1 clove garlic, minced
- 1 skinless, boneless chicken breast half - cut
- 2 leaves bok choy, diced
- 1/4 cup chicken broth
- 2 tablespoons dry sherry
- 1 tablespoon soy sauce
- 1 1/2 tablespoons hoisin sauce
- 1/8 teaspoon salt

into bite-size pieces

- 1 tablespoon grated fresh ginger
- 2 green onions, minced

DIRECTIONS

1. In a large pot with boiling salted water cook angel hair pasta until al dente. Drain.
2. Meanwhile, in a large nonstick skillet heat canola and sesame oil over medium high heat. Saute onion and garlic until softened. Stir in chopped chicken, and cook until chicken browns and juices run clear. Stir in ginger, bok choy, chicken stock, sherry, soy sauce, and hoisin sauce. Reduce heat, and continue cooking for 10 minutes.
3. Toss pasta with chicken mixture until well coated. Season with salt. Serve warm sprinkled with minced green onions.

ROASTED TURKEY LEGS

Servings: 3 | Prep: 15m | Cooks: 2h | Total: 2h15m

NUTRITION FACTS

Calories: 643.1 | Carbohydrates: 1.2g | Protein: 73.1g | Cholesterol: 239.4mg | Sodium: 399.4mg

INGREDIENTS

- 3 stalks celery stalks, cut in thirds
- 3 turkey legs
- 6 tablespoons butter
- 1 pinch salt to taste
- 1/2 cup water, or as needed

DIRECTIONS

1. Preheat the oven to 350 degrees F (175 degrees C). Rinse the turkey legs and pat dry.
2. Stand the turkey legs upright (as if the turkey were standing). Press a knife downward into the deep tissue, creating 2 or 3 long pockets. Press a piece of celery into each opening. Pull back the skin on the legs, rub with butter, and season with a little salt. Put the skin back into place, rub with more butter, and season lightly with salt. Lay the legs in a roasting pan.
3. Roast uncovered for 1 1/2 to 2 hours, until the legs are golden brown and the internal temperature is 180 degrees F (82 degrees C) when taken with a meat thermometer. Add more water if needed while roasting, and baste occasionally with the juices or butter.

BROWN RICE BREAKFAST PORRIDGE

Servings: 2 | Prep: 5m | Cooks: 25m | Total: 30m

NUTRITION FACTS

Calories: 318.3 | Carbohydrates: 44.7g | Protein: 9.9g | Cholesterol: 118mg | Sodium: 130.3mg

INGREDIENTS

- 1 cup cooked brown rice
- 1 cup 2% low-fat milk
- 2 tablespoons dried blueberries
- 1 dash cinnamon
- 1 tablespoon honey
- 1 egg
- 1/4 teaspoon vanilla extract
- 1 tablespoon butter

DIRECTIONS

1. Combine the cooked brown rice, milk, blueberries, cinnamon, and honey in a small saucepan. Bring to a boil, then reduce heat to low and simmer for 20 minutes.
2. Beat the egg in a small bowl. Temper the egg by whisking in some of the hot rice, a tablespoon at a time until you have incorporated about 6 tablespoons. Stir the egg into the rice along with the vanilla and butter, and continue cooking over low heat for 1 to 2 minutes to thicken.

SAVANNAH'S BEST MARINATED PORTOBELLO MUSHROOMS

Servings: 2 | Prep: 10m | Cooks: 33m | Total: 1h | Additional: 17m

NUTRITION FACTS

Calories: 112.4 | Carbohydrates: 4.5g | Protein: 1.3g | Cholesterol: 0mg | | Sodium: 1286mg

INGREDIENTS

- 1/2 cup cooking wine
- 1 tablespoon olive oil
- 2 tablespoons dark soy sauce
- 2 tablespoons balsamic vinegar
- 2 cloves garlic, minced
- 2 large portobello mushroom caps

DIRECTIONS

1. Preheat oven to 400 degrees F (200 degrees C).
2. In a baking dish, mix the wine, olive oil, soy sauce, balsamic vinegar, and garlic. Place mushroom caps upside down in the marinade, and marinate 15 minutes.
3. Cover dish, and transfer to the preheated oven. Bake 25 minutes. Turn mushrooms and continue baking 8 minutes.

SALMON MANGO BANGO

Servings: 2 | Prep: 10m | Cooks: 5m | Total: 30m | Additional: 15m

NUTRITION FACTS

Calories: 307 | Carbohydrates: 27g | Fat: 11.6g | Protein: 25.1g | Cholesterol: 51mg | Sodium: 211mg

INGREDIENTS

- 1 mango - peeled, seeded and diced
- 2 tablespoons lime juice
- 2 tablespoons red bell pepper and ancho chili pepper jam
- 2 tablespoons chopped fresh cilantro
- 2 salmon fillets, skin removed
- sea salt to taste
- 2 teaspoons vegetable oil

DIRECTIONS

1. Stir mango, lime juice, pepper jam, and cilantro together in a bowl. Cover the bowl and refrigerate for relish flavors to combine, about 30 minutes.
2. Season salmon fillets with sea salt.
3. Heat oil in a large non-stick skillet over medium-high heat until oil begins to smoke. Place salmon, flesh-side down, in the hot skillet and cook until edges are just starting to cook through, about 2 minutes. Flip fillets, remove skillet from heat, and let fillets sit in the hot pan until cooked through, 2 to 3 minutes more. Transfer to a plate and top with chilled mango relish.

FRUITY GRILLED PORK TENDERLOIN

Servings: 2 | Prep: 15m | Cooks: 30m | Total: 4h45m | Additional: 4h

NUTRITION FACTS

Calories: 543.5 | Carbohydrates: 85.1g | Protein: 37.3g | Cholesterol: 98.2mg | Sodium: 1918.9mg

INGREDIENTS

- 1/4 cup soy sauce
- 1/3 cup packed brown sugar
- 1/3 cup plum jam
- 3/4 cup black cherry soda
- 1 (1 pound) pork tenderloin

DIRECTIONS

1. In a small sauce pan, mix together soy sauce, brown sugar, and jam over low heat until sugar has dissolved. Reserve 1/4 cup of sauce for basting the tenderloin while grilling. Combine remaining sauce with soda in a large plastic resealable bag; place meat in bag, and seal. Marinate in the refrigerator for at least 4 hours, or overnight.
2. Preheat grill for medium heat.
3. Lightly oil preheated grill, and discard marinade. Cook tenderloin for 15 to 20 minutes, or until an instant-read thermometer inserted into the center reads 145 degrees F (63 degrees C).
4. Remove meat from grill, and allow to rest for 5 minutes before slicing into 1/4 inch thick medallions.

NEW ORLEANS BARBEQUED SHRIMP

Servings: 2 | Prep: 10m | Cooks: 30m | Total: 40m

NUTRITION FACTS

Calories: 871.1 | Carbohydrates: 7.7g | Protein: 47.1g | Cholesterol: 467.1mg | Sodium: 1666.1mg

INGREDIENTS

- 1 pound shrimp, heads off and unpeeled
- 1/2 cup butter
- 1/2 cup zesty Italian dressing
- 1 tablespoon lemon juice
- 2 teaspoons ground black pepper
- 1/8 teaspoon garlic powder

DIRECTIONS

1. Preheat oven to 350 degrees F (175 degrees C).
2. Wash shrimp and drain well.
3. Melt margarine/butter in a one quart casserole dish. Add salad dressing, lemon juice, black pepper and garlic powder.

4. Add shrimp to the casserole dish. Stir gently to cover the shrimp with the mixture. Cover and bake, stirring occasionally for 25 to 30 minutes or until shrimp are pink.
5. Serve the shrimp hot on a large platter and place the sauce in individual bowls so that you can easily 'dunk' bread in the sauce!

E-Z MARINATED SWORDFISH

Servings: 2 | Prep: 10m | Cooks: 10m | Total: 30m | Additional: 10m

NUTRITION FACTS

Calories: 353.5 | Carbohydrates: 2.4g | Protein: 27.2g | Cholesterol: 53mg | Sodium: 1302.5mg

INGREDIENTS

- 3 tablespoons fresh lime juice
- 2 tablespoons white wine vinegar
- 1 teaspoon salt
- 1/8 teaspoon freshly ground black pepper
- 1/4 teaspoon ground ginger
- 1/4 teaspoon dried basil
- 1/8 teaspoon dried thyme
- 1/8 teaspoon dried parsley
- 1 teaspoon hot pepper sauce
- 1 pinch cayenne pepper
- 3 tablespoons vegetable oil
- 2 piece (4-1/2" x 2-1/8" x 7/8")s fresh swordfish fillets

DIRECTIONS

1. In a medium bowl, stir together the lime juice, white wine vinegar, salt, pepper, ginger, basil, thyme, parsley, hot pepper sauce, cayenne pepper, and oil. Place the fish fillets into the bowl, cover, and marinate for at least 10 minutes, or preferably up to 3 hours.
2. Preheat broiler or an outdoor grill for high heat.
3. Place fish onto the grill or a broiling pan. Discard marinade. Grill or broil fish about five minutes each side, until the fish flakes easily with a fork.

MOZZARELLA MUSHROOM CHICKEN

Servings: 2 | Prep: 15m | Cooks: 30m | Total: 45m

NUTRITION FACTS

Calories: 641.8 | Carbohydrates: 8.8g | Protein: 56.3g | Cholesterol: 144.3mg | Sodium: 766.4mg

INGREDIENTS

- 3 tablespoons olive oil
- 2 skinless, boneless chicken breast halves
- 1 tablespoon garlic powder
- 1 clove garlic, minced
- 6 fresh mushrooms, sliced
- 2 cups shredded mozzarella cheese

DIRECTIONS

1. Heat the olive oil in a skillet over medium heat. Place chicken in the skillet, and season with garlic powder and garlic. Cook 12 minutes on each side, or until juices run clear. Set chicken aside, and keep warm.
2. Stir mushrooms into the skillet, and cook until tender. Return chicken to skillet, layer with mushrooms, and top with cheese. Cover skillet, and continue cooking 5 minutes, or until cheese is melted.

HAM AND CHICKEN CASSEROLE

Servings: 2 | Prep: 20m | Cooks: 35m | Total: 55m

NUTRITION FACTS

Calories: 514.2 | Carbohydrates: 20.7g | Protein: 33.4g | Cholesterol: 20.7mg | Sodium: 1166.4mg

INGREDIENTS

- 1/2 cup uncooked egg noodles
- 2 tablespoons butter
- 2 tablespoons all-purpose flour
- 1 cup milk
- 1/2 cup cooked, cubed chicken breast meat
- 1/2 cup cooked, diced ham
- 1/4 cup chopped celery
- 1/4 teaspoon salt
- 1/4 teaspoon ground black pepper
- 3 ounces shredded Cheddar cheese
- 1 teaspoon paprika

DIRECTIONS

1. Preheat oven to 400 degrees F (200 degrees C). Lightly grease a medium baking dish.
2. Bring a saucepan of lightly salted water to a boil. Cook egg noodles in boiling water for 6 to 8 minutes, or until al dente. Drain.

3. Melt butter in a saucepan over medium-low heat. Mix in flour, heating until bubbly. Slowly whisk in milk. Cook for 5 minutes, stirring constantly, or until thick and smooth. Remove the saucepan from heat. Mix in the noodles, chicken, ham, celery, salt, and pepper. Spoon the mixture into the prepared baking dish.
4. Bake for 15 minutes in the preheated oven. Sprinkle with cheese and paprika, and continue baking for another 5 minutes. Serve hot!

VEAL CHOP WITH PORTABELLO MUSHROOMS

Servings: 2 | Prep: 15m | Cooks: 25m | Total: 40m

NUTRITION FACTS

Calories: 554.9 | Carbohydrates: 5.2g | Protein: 21.7g | Cholesterol: 97.5mg | Sodium: 838.4mg

INGREDIENTS

- 5 tablespoons olive oil, divided
- 1 tablespoon butter
- 2 raw chop with refuse, 195 g; yields excluding refuses veal chops
- 1 portobello mushroom, sliced
- 1 1/2 cups chicken broth
- 1 1/2 teaspoons fresh rosemary, chopped
- 1/2 cup red wine

DIRECTIONS

1. Heat 4 tablespoons olive oil with butter in a skillet over medium-high heat. Cook chops until browned, 2 to 3 minutes per side.
2. Once browned, stir in mushrooms and cook for 1 minute. Add chicken broth and rosemary; cover, and simmer 10 minutes. Stir in red wine, increase heat, and cook, uncovered, until sauce is reduced by half. Veal chops may be removed at any time to prevent over-cooking, then returned to the pan for the final minute.
3. Drizzle with remaining 1 tablespoon olive oil, and serve.

ZUCCHINI E POMODORI GRATINATI (ZUCCHINI AND TOMATO GRATIN)

Servings: 2 | Prep: 15m | Cooks: 45m | Total: 1h

NUTRITION FACTS

Calories: 412.2 | Carbohydrates: 24.9g | Protein: 23.8g | Cholesterol: 43.5mg | Sodium: 563.1mg

INGREDIENTS

- 2 tablespoons olive oil
- 4 eaches zucchini, sliced
- 1 large clove garlic, crushed
- 4 ounces thinly sliced mozzarella cheese
- 4 large tomatoes, peeled and sliced
- 1/4 cup grated Parmesan cheese
- 1 tablespoon chopped fresh basil
- 1 pinch salt and freshly ground black pepper

DIRECTIONS

1. Preheat oven to 375 degrees F (190 degrees C). Move oven rack into the top third of the oven.
2. Heat the olive oil in a large skillet over medium heat, and spread the zucchini slices into the skillet in a single layer. If they don't fit, cook them in batches. Sprinkle pieces of garlic over the zucchini, and cook until the zucchini are golden brown on both sides, about 8 minutes per side. Remove from heat.
3. Arrange the slices of zucchini in an 9x12-inch glass baking dish, alternating with slices of mozzarella cheese and tomato, so that the slices overlap each other in a neat row pattern. Sprinkle the Parmesan cheese and basil over the dish, and season to taste with salt and pepper.
4. Bake in the preheated oven until the cheese is melted and brown and the dish is bubbling, about 30 minutes.

GRILLED SALMON STEAKS WITH SAVORY BLUEBERRY SAUCE

Servings: 4 | Prep: 10m | Cooks: 15m | Total: 25m

NUTRITION FACTS

Calories: 383.2 | Carbohydrates: 12.8g | Protein: 26.9g | Cholesterol: 83.5mg | Sodium: 264.7mg

INGREDIENTS

- 1/2 cup chicken stock
- 1/4 cup balsamic vinegar
- 1/4 cup orange juice
- 1 teaspoon honey
- 1 tablespoon cornstarch
- 1/4 cup chicken stock
- 1 cup fresh blueberries
- 2 teaspoons chopped fresh chives
- 4 (6 ounce) salmon steaks
- 2 tablespoons olive oil
- 1 pinch salt and pepper to taste

DIRECTIONS

1. Pour 1/2 cup chicken stock, vinegar, orange juice, and honey into a saucepan. Bring to a boil over high heat, then reduce heat to medium. Dissolve cornstarch in 1/4 cup of chicken stock, and stir into the simmering sauce. Cook and stir until the sauce thickens and turns clear, 1 to 2 minutes. Stir in the blueberries and chives, and keep warm over low heat.
2. Preheat grill to medium high-heat.
3. Brush salmon with oil, and season to taste with salt and pepper. Grill until the fish flakes easily with a fork, about 3 to 4 minutes per side. Serve with blueberry sauce.

SEA BASS A LA MICHELE

Servings: 2 | Prep: 10m | Cooks: 15m | Total: 25m

NUTRITION FACTS

Calories: 561 | Carbohydrates: 50.6g | Fat: 18.5g | Protein: 46.9g | Cholesterol: 94mg | Sodium: 1131mg

INGREDIENTS

- 2 tablespoons olive oil, plus more for drizzling
- 2 tablespoons sherry vinegar
- 1 teaspoon smoked paprika, plus more for topping
- 1 teaspoon kosher salt, plus more to taste
- 1/2 cup sliced green onions
- 1 red jalapeno pepper, sliced
- 4 small potatoes, quartered
- 2 (8 ounce) thick-cut boneless, skinless Chilean sea bass fillets

DIRECTIONS

1. Preheat oven to 450 degrees F (230 degrees C). Oil a baking dish.
2. Microwave potatoes in a microwave dish on High until just softened, about 5 minutes.
3. Whisk olive oil and sherry vinegar together in a bowl. Add smoked paprika and salt; whisk to blend. Stir in onions, red jalapeno, and cooked potatoes. Slide the fish fillets into the mixture, turning and coating them with the vinaigrette. Remove the fish from potato mixture.
4. Place potatoes in prepared baking dish. Nestle fish onto potatoes. Sprinkle with a pinch of salt, a dash of paprika, and a drizzle of olive oil.
5. Bake in center of preheated oven until just cooked through and fish flakes easily, about 15 minutes.

RISOTTO WITH CHICKEN AND ASPARAGUS

Servings: 2 | Prep: 20m | Cooks: 40m | Total: 1h

NUTRITION FACTS

Calories: 877.3 | Carbohydrates: 104.7g | Protein: 50.8g | Cholesterol: 104.3mg | Sodium: 1074mg

INGREDIENTS

- 2 cups chicken stock
- 1 tablespoon olive oil or butter
- 1 tablespoon minced garlic
- 2 (5 ounce) skinless, boneless chicken breast halves - cubed
- 2 teaspoons olive oil or butter
- 1/2 large onion, minced
- 1 cup Carnaroli or Arborio rice
- 1/2 cup white wine
- 8 ounces asparagus, finely chopped
- 1/2 teaspoon dried oregano
- 1/2 teaspoon dried basil
- 1 pinch salt and freshly ground black pepper to taste
- 1/2 cup freshly grated Parmesan cheese

DIRECTIONS

1. Bring chicken stock to a boil in a small saucepan, then keep warm over low heat.
2. Heat 1 teaspoon olive oil in a large saucepan over medium-high heat. Stir in the garlic and cook 30 seconds until fragrant. Add the cubed chicken, and continue cooking until firm and lightly browned; set aside.
3. Heat remaining 2 teaspoons olive oil in the saucepan and cook onions until they soften and turn translucent, about 1 minute. Stir in the rice, and continue cooking until the rice turns opaque, and the onion begins to brown.
4. Stir in the wine and asparagus; cook, stirring constantly, until the wine evaporates. Reduce heat to medium, and stir in 1/3 of the hot chicken stock. Cook, stirring constantly, until all of the liquid has been absorbed, 8 to 10 minutes.
5. Stir in another 1/3 of the chicken stock and continue cooking and stirring until absorbed, 8 to 10 minutes. Season the risotto with oregano and basil. Pour in the remaining stock, and stir until absorbed again, 8 to 10 minutes. Season to taste with salt and pepper, then stir in the Parmesan cheese and chicken cubes.

TERIYAKI RIB EYE STEAKS

Servings: 2 | Prep: 10m | Cooks: 15m | Total: 2h25m | Additional: 2h

NUTRITION FACTS

Calories: 297.1 | Carbohydrates: 13.5g | Protein: 19.6g | Cholesterol: 60.3mg | Sodium: 991.6mg

INGREDIENTS

- 2 tablespoons soy sauce
- 2 tablespoons water
- 1 tablespoon white sugar
- 1 1/2 teaspoons honey
- 1 1/2 teaspoons Worcestershire sauce
- 1 1/4 teaspoons distilled white vinegar
- 1 teaspoon olive oil
- 1/4 teaspoon onion powder
- 1/4 teaspoon garlic powder
- 1/8 teaspoon ground ginger
- 2 (6 ounce) lean beef rib eye steaks

DIRECTIONS

1. Whisk together the soy sauce, water, sugar, honey, Worcestershire sauce, vinegar, olive oil, onion powder, garlic powder, and ground ginger in a large bowl. Pierce steaks several times with a fork. Marinate steaks in soy sauce mixture for at least 2 hours.
2. Cook the steaks in a hot skillet, wok, or hibachi over medium heat; 7 minutes per side for medium. An instant-read thermometer inserted into the center should read 140 degrees F (60 degrees C).

STUFFED PORK CHOPS WITH GORGONZOLA AND APPLE

Servings: 2 | Prep: 45m | Cooks: 1h | Total: 1h45m

NUTRITION FACTS

Calories: 420.4 | Carbohydrates: 9.4g | Protein: 23.5g | Cholesterol: 117.7mg | Sodium: 623.3mg

INGREDIENTS

- 1 tablespoon butter
- 1/2 tablespoon dried thyme
- 2 cloves garlic
- 1/4 cup Gorgonzola cheese

- 1/2 cup chopped Granny Smith apples
- ground black pepper to taste
- 1/4 cup Gorgonzola cheese at room temperature, crumbled
- 2 thick cut pork chops
- 1/2 teaspoon olive oil
- 3 tablespoons dry sherry
- 1/8 cup heavy cream
- 1/2 cup chicken broth
- salt and pepper to taste

DIRECTIONS

1. Preheat oven to 375 degrees F (190 degrees C).
2. To make the apple stuffing: In a saute pan or skillet on medium heat, melt the butter and saute thyme, chopped apples, salt and pepper together until the apples are completely softened; about 15 to 20 minutes.
3. Place the apple mixture in a bowl and mix in 1/4 cup Gorgonzola cheese. The cheese should liquefy into the stuffing within a couple of minutes.
4. To prepare the pork chops: Butterfly the pork chops by slicing them parallel to the plane of the chop from the fat side to the bone. Stuff each one with about 2 to 3 tablespoons of the apple mixture.
5. Bake the chops for about 1 hour. Place the chops on a rack with the two stuffing sides pressed together to hold the stuffing inside the chops.
6. To make the sauce: Heat the oil in a saute pan or skillet on medium heat, then saute the garlic until transparent, and the cheese until slightly melting. Immediately add the sherry, let cook for a minute until combined, then add the cream and 1/4 cup of the chicken stock, salt and pepper. Stir until well blended. Stir occasionally and reduce the liquid on medium high heat until the sauce begins to toast/caramelize and turn darker brown. Add the remaining 1/4 cup chicken stock, reincorporate the cheese and continue reducing until there is just 1/4 to 1/2 cup of thick liquid remaining.

BEEF AND MUSHROOM STUFFED PEPPERS

Servings: 3 | Prep: 20m | Cooks: 30m | Total: 50m

NUTRITION FACTS

Calories: 600.4 | Carbohydrates: 17.6g | Protein: 36.7g | Cholesterol: 121.7mg | Sodium: 1280.8mg

INGREDIENTS

- 1 pound ground beef
- 1 cup fresh mushrooms, sliced
- salt and pepper to taste
- 3 small red bell peppers, halved and seeded

- 1/2 white onion, diced
- 2 cups beef gravy

- 3/4 cup shredded Monterey Jack cheese

DIRECTIONS

1. Preheat oven to 375 degrees F (190 degrees C).
2. Brown beef in a large skillet over medium-high heat. Halfway through browning, add mushrooms and onion. Continue cooking until meat is fully browned; drain fat from skillet. Stir in enough gravy to bond mixture without making it soupy. Season with salt and pepper, and set aside.
3. Meanwhile, heat a medium saucepan of water until boiling. Place peppers in water, and boil for 2 to 3 minutes, until just tender; remove from water. Place peppers, hollow side up, in a 9x13 inch baking dish, and fill each with beef mixture.
4. Bake in preheated oven for 15 to 20 minutes, until bubbling. Top with cheese, and bake for an additional 5 to 10 minutes. Serve in a small pool of gravy.

CREAMY COTTAGE CHEESE SCRAMBLED EGGS

Servings: 2 | Prep: 5m | Cooks: 5m | Total: 10m

NUTRITION FACTS

Calories: 224.3 | Carbohydrates: 1.9g | Protein: 16.2g | Cholesterol: 391.5mg | Sodium: 295mg

INGREDIENTS

- 1 tablespoon butter
- 4 eggs, beaten
- 1/4 cup cottage cheese

- 1 pinch ground black pepper to taste
- 1 teaspoon chopped fresh chives, or to taste

DIRECTIONS

1. Melt butter in a skillet over medium heat. Pour beaten eggs into the skillet; let cook undisturbed until the bottom of the eggs begin to firm, 1 to 2 minutes.
2. Stir cottage cheese and chives into eggs and season with black pepper. Cook and stir until eggs are nearly set, 3 to 4 minutes more.

BAKED SHELLS IN SAUCE

Servings: 2 | Prep: 10m | Cooks: 30m | Total: 40m

NUTRITION FACTS

Calories: 212.4 | Carbohydrates: 29.5g | Protein: 13.3g | Cholesterol: 13.4mg | Sodium: 818.8mg

INGREDIENTS

- 1/2 cup seashell pasta
- 1 cup tomato sauce
- 1/2 cup mushrooms, diced
- 1/4 cup crumbled firm silken tofu
- 1/4 cup shredded mozzarella cheese
- 2 tablespoons grated Parmesan cheese

DIRECTIONS

1. Bring a pot of lightly salted water to a boil. Add pasta and cook for 8 to 10 minutes or until al dente; drain.
2. Preheat oven to 400 degrees F (200 degrees C).
3. In a medium bowl combine tomato sauce, mushrooms and tofu. Stir in cooked pasta. In a separate, small bowl combine mozzarella and Parmesan cheeses.
4. In a small casserole dish layer pasta mixture and cheeses.
5. Bake in preheated oven for 30 minutes, or until lightly browned.